RICHARD CRASHAW

A STUDY IN
BAROQUE SENSIBILITY

RICHARD CRASHAW

A Study in Baroque Sensibility

BY AUSTIN WARREN

ANN ARBOR BOOKS
THE UNIVERSITY OF MICHIGAN PRESS

FOR

BENJAMIN AND EDMUND

PREFACE

WHAT IS the meaning of a poem? Assuredly no age has developed such scrupulosity concerning the reply as ours. Like other questions unasked by common sense but, if raised, innocently answered, this question has produced, among contemporary critics, difficulty amounting to scepticism. The solipsist answer, "As many meanings as there are readers," is the simplest and is, as a description of normal experience, the most accurate; but that is simply to reduce the poem to an "event" and its meaning to the natural associations it arouses in the consciousness and subconsciousness of the reader; it is, in effect, to reduce the poem to its subject, or supposed subject (e.g., God, trees, the death of a beautiful woman), upon which, started off by a few rhythmic chords from the poet's lyre, the reader allows himself an agreeable reverie. Yet whatever else it may offer, the special virtue of poetry must be attached to words, its medium, so that if one gains from the reading of a poem no more than that incitation to ruminate provided by a photograph or a tune, one is —to say the least—failing to make efficient use of the special art. The fundamental value or "absolute" of the poem must lie in what a poet can offer—his rhythms and images, the values which, by selection and juxtaposition, he gives to words, the organic "meaning" of rhythm, image, and word as begot by the "maker."

This meaning can be added to or enriched—only the additions must, like Grieg's second-piano accompaniment to the Mozart Sonatas, fill in, not cancel, the original. I do not say that we can ever reconstruct, perfectly, the author's meaning; nor that ours should be the purist aim of mere reconstruction, "mere" restoration of Shakespeare to Elizabethan psychology and Elizabethan dramaturgy; nor that alert sensibility is not often able to supply what erudition may long seek and at length but tentatively provide. Poetry is endowed with multiple meanings as with multiple attractions. Like Mr. Eliot, I begin—and think it well for readers to begin —by liking the sound of poetry or being arrested by its images before I care to explore its total significance; and poetry offers much merely as a kind of music. But the full experience of poetry is something again, as poetry is less and more than painting, less and more than music; and its meaning is finally the apprehension and re-creation of its author's meaning (percepts, concepts, words, rhythms, images in fusion) by means of whatever in the reader's experience is consonant, and augmented (if possible) by whatever in his experience, alien to the poet's, can be brought into focus with it.

Most voluntary readers have, undoubtedly, in every age restricted themselves to the poetry contemporary with themselves, and for obvious reasons. The re-creation of poetry written in the past requires some history to be provided, either by our own labor or that of others. Erudition must affix glossaries, explain allusions, supply the stylistic and ideological environment before either the aesthetic experience or the critical judgment can, with surety, operate.

This study chiefly addresses itself to translating the twentieth-century reader of Crashaw into the position of one who, three centuries ago, was informed upon the principal movements in English and Continental religion and art, and conversant with Latin, Italian, and English poetry. The translation can never be complete, but to the extent that it is incomplete, the *communication* between Crashaw and us is imperfect, and to that extent we do not receive *his* poem but intercalate parts of our own. It is the humble use of scholarship to ensure, so far as its knowledge extends, that when we read the poetry of three centuries ago we attain the *poet's* meaning.

Such a conception of meaning leads—like the contrary belief, that there are as many meanings as readers—to an infinite regress, an absurd reduction. Since the experience which readers bring to their reading augments, and since their moods and environments vary, there are as many meanings not as readers but as readings: with my growth, Milton expands; the meaning of Henry James in a mill town differs, by the exclusions made palpable, from what it incorporates for Edith Wharton. On the other hand, if *meaning* be the author's, only the author—and the author at the moment of composition—can supply us with the genetic history of incitation, intent, the contents of his consciousness and subconsciousness, what was expressed, what implied, what, deliberately or instinctively, excluded. Scholarship can but clumsily try to establish the date at which a poem was composed, and what, before and concurrently, was the movement of the poet's outer life of action and inner life of reaction. Yet we can acquire certain sorts of relevant information which a poet's contemporaries often lacked. Thus the recent biographies of Hart Crane and E. A. Robinson have made Crane's meaning and Robinson's meaning apprehensible in certain important respects as they were not during the poets' lives, even to their acquaintances. Scant as is our knowledge of Crashaw's career, we know considerably more than did his readers in 1642, most of whom, outside of Cambridge, can have known only what the preface to *Steps* told of this "Learned young Gent. (now dead to us)." Is it relevant to the apprehension of Crashaw's *meaning* to know that he was reared by a father who spent his days and his learning on the hatred of Catholicism, or that Crashaw, after leaving Puritanism for the Laudian sacramentalism, finally made his submission to Rome? No one of these facts can be learned *from* his poems, all of which might have been written by one who, like Joseph Beaumont, lived and died a High Anglican; yet all that a man is at the moment when he writes a poem goes into its meaning for him; and if the meaning, for the reader, is to be the author's in some ampler sense than that of attaching his language to the denotation prescribed by the *New Oxford Dictionary* as approximately of his date, such extrapoetic information seems requisite.

Of the many obligations which I have incurred during my study, I must acknowledge first the generosity of the American Council of Learned Societies, as whose Fellow I was enabled to spend a year in England. The British Museum, the Bodleian, the University Library at Cambridge and those of Peterhouse and St. John's, the McAlpin Collection of the Union Theological Seminary, and the Widener Library of Harvard University: all have my thanks for extended courtesies. Among scholars, the late Rev. Thomas A. Walker, historian of Peterhouse; Mr. Herbert Butterfield, Librarian of Peterhouse; Mr. Aubrey Attwater, late Librarian of Pembroke; Mr. E. A. B. Barnard, F. R. Hist. S., historian of Little St. Mary's; the Vicar of Little St. Mary's (Fr. Hankey); and Mr. Leonard Whibley, of Pembroke, have helped me by information and by access to manuscript records. To Mr. T. S. Eliot, I am indebted for hospitality, good will, and, above all, for the stimulus of his thought concerning seventeenth-century poetry. No one can write on Crashaw without obligation to Professor L. C. Martin and to Dr. Mario Praz, and both have given me encouragement: to Dr. Praz I owe especial thanks for long-continued and various assistance.

At secretarial offices, the Misses Murphy, Lydon, Baron, and Nanscawen have labored faithfully. Eleanor Mitchell, Milford Wence, Edmund Halsey —friends, and readers of the manuscript—made sound criticisms which I have endeavored to heed. Miss Ruth Wallerstein kindly let me profit from her sensitive criticism of Crashaw while it was still awaiting publication. The Rev. Benjamin Bissell, who long ago introduced me to Crashaw, and who now lives in Crashaw's Cambridge, has responded promptly to every trans-Atlantic call for assistance. Lastly, I gratefully avow large debt to the sensibility and critical wits of my friend, Howard Blake.

A. W.

Boston
21 December 1938

CONTENTS

CONTENTS

RICHARD CRASHAW

A STUDY IN
BAROQUE SENSIBILITY

CHAPTER ONE

THE LAUDIAN MOVEMENT AND THE COUNTER-REFORMATION

RELIGION, for the seventeenth century, had lost none of its dominance over the intellect, the emotions, and the imagination. The ardors of Reformist zeal had not wholly spent themselves; and, since the Council of Trent, the Catholic Church had exhibited, in learned argument against heretics and schismatics, in missionary exploits, in devotional life, and in the arts, a persistent and passionate activity.

The seventeenth century was the Golden Age of the Anglican Church: it dominated the intellectual life of England, included within its communion scholars like Ussher, Burton, Evelyn, Selden, and attracted to it such as Casaubon; it produced such preachers as Andrewes, Donne, and Taylor; it harbored the sceptical fideism of the *Religio Medici;* and it expressed itself in religious poetry as various as that of George Herbert, Joseph Beaumont, Quarles, and Vaughan.

Then, as now, the Church was comprehensive. In the seventeenth century, the Establishment housed the High, the Low, the Broad—or, as they then were termed, the Laudians, the Puritans, and the

"Latitude men." Such generosity produced inevitable tension. The Marian exiles, who had returned from Geneva, thoroughly converted to Calvinistic theology, were zealous to purge their own communion of its lingering superstitions and to refashion it after a truly evangelical pattern; and, during the reign of Elizabeth, they largely dominated the national theology. But, with the early years of the new century, there appeared a more or less coherent group of divines who, while rejecting papal claims and the more recent developments of Italian and Spanish theology, and admitting the need for a purification of medieval practices, felt themselves and their Church to be Catholic. It may be fairly said that Anglicanism in the seventeenth century represented two genuine pieties, one looking to Geneva and the other, though with cautious reservations, to its own pre-Reformation past and Rome's, and that the religious wars of Europe, the conflicts between Catholics and Protestants, found epitomized representation in that century-long conflict between the Puritans and the Orthodox of which the Civil War was but the concentrated and palpable episode. The rise of the Laudian party, in reaction against the school of Geneva, parallels, in miniature, the ascending movement of the Counter-Reformation.[1]

In 1611, William Laud was appointed chaplain to the King; in 1620, he conducted, before King James, the King's favorite, the Duke of Buckingham, and

Buckingham's mother, his famous conference with the Jesuit, Fisher; thereafter, he became Buckingham's confessor. The accession of King Charles, amateur theologian and cultivated gentleman, submitted the country to the control of Buckingham and of his confessor, for whom Charles felt a high and constant respect. While still Bishop of Bath, Laud had drawn up a list of clergy for the use of the King, marking the "Orthodox" for promotion and the Puritans for neglect. Raised to the throne of Canterbury in 1633, and supported by men of like convictions in most of the episcopal sees, he was able to prosecute a "thorough" discipline of the clergy and church life. During the decade when no Parliament sat, Laud, whose rigor was as sincere as tactless, ruled ecclesiastical affairs.[2]

Neither a bigot nor obscurantist, Laud munificently patronized the universities; and his conference with Fisher exhibits him as an able apologist. The English Church, for Laud, was Catholic yet reformed, the *via media* between Geneva and Rome. He proclaimed an inclusive gospel. "The Catholic Church of Christ is neither Rome nor a conventicle. Out of that there is no salvation, I easily confess it. But out of Rome there is, and out of conventicle too; salvation is not shut up into such a narrow conclave."[3]

This inclusive theology was, however, not calculated to recommend the Primate to the Puritans, insistent upon doctrinal precision; and his determina-

tion to enforce a moderate uniformity in the ordering
of churches and their ceremonial met with equally
determined nonconformity.

Under Laud's administration, party feeling within
the Church grew violent, both in the universities and
in the city. London remained strongly Puritan: and,
at Cambridge, in the unconsecrated chapels of Em-
manuel and Sidney Sussex, unsurpliced clergy conducted services of their own devisings. Meanwhile
there developed a party of zealous Arminians, among
whom were young men of more enthusiasm than
perspective—ritualists and bigots who exposed the
whole party to the charge of Romanizing.[4] That the
movement led many to Popery may confidently be
denied; but, like the Oxford Movement of the nineteenth century, it assuredly sought to restore what it
regarded as the traditional heritage of the Anglican
Church; and it is clear, too, that it attracted much
the same types of persons as did the later movement.

The Laudian clergy protested against the lax
etiquette of their congregations; and they sought,
some by persuasion, some by compulsion, to establish
habits of reverence. They railed in the communion
tables at the east end; some of them introduced stone
altars. These innovations angered the Puritans, and
still more did the genuflection to the altar enjoined
upon those entering a church.[5]

The church buildings, which had fallen into neglect and decay during the age of Elizabeth, were an
object of concern to the Laudian clergy. In the

Catholic spirit, they taught their people that "too much cost cannot be bestowed on Christ" and that His Temple should be grander than houses of men.

They exalted the Sacraments. Though accused of teaching, in his *Book of Devotions*, that there were seven, Cosin was careful to distinguish the "two chief" from those others which the Prayer Book calls rites;[6] but in Shelford's *Discourses* the Catholic seven appear without distinction. "Desire you new life? here is Baptisme to give it. Are you gone from it? here is the Baptisme of tears and pennance to restore it[Confession]. Want you weapons for the spirituall warre? here is the Catechisme, and Confirmation. Need you food for the new life? here is the bread and wine of Christ's body and blood. Want you supply of vertuous young souldiers? here is Matrimonie and Christian education. Need you leaders and governours? here are Christ's ministers. Want you provision for the journey to the high Jerusalem? here is the viaticum of the heavenly manna expressed in the communion of the sick." The Sacraments, this Anglican rector further taught, are not, as the Puritans believed, mere sign and symbols: "Christ's Sacraments bestow," they "infuse," grace.[7]

Though they rejected Transubstantiation as a speculative philosophic theory of how the elements became sacramental, the Laudians preached the Real Presence of Christ in the Blessed Sacrament, adding, sometimes, that in so doing they were preaching not Roman doctrine but doctrine common to Luther and

Calvin and indeed most Protestants. Lancelot Andrewes, addressing Cardinal Bellarmine, expounded
the classic position of his school: "As to the Real
Presence, we are agreed; our controversy is as to the
mode of it. The Presence we believe to be real, as you
do. As to the mode we define nothing rashly, nor
anxiously investigate. . . ." [8]

The Laudians revived auricular confession, permitted but not required by Anglican formularies.
Some of the more fanatic insisted upon it as requisite
to a good communion. In 1637, two vigorous sermons
in advocacy were preached at Cambridge by Anthony
Sparrow of Queens and Sylvester Adams of Peterhouse; [9] and Cosin, defending Adams' doctrine,
wrote: "Such confession was in use even from Apostolic times, and the Church of England hath not
abrogated it, except in some additiments and circumstances, not in substance or essence." [10] Jeremy Taylor
was "ghostly father" to John Evelyn; Laud, the confessor to the King and the Duke of Buckingham.
From enrollment in a profession, Holy Orders grew
sacerdotal; and, to the horror of the Puritans, the use
of the term *priest* was revived. [11]

Celibacy received new honor and respect. Andrewes
gives thanks, in his *Devotions,* for

> The ascetics and their tears,
> The virgins, flowers of purity,
>   Celestial gems,
>   Brides of the Immaculate Lamb.

Himself a celibate, Laud announced his intention to prefer, when abilities were equal, unmarried over married priests. In his *Holy Living,* Jeremy Taylor exalted virginity, and included a special "prayer for the Love of God, to be said by Virgins and Widows, professed or resolved so to live. . . ." [12]

The saints were given new honor in art and poetry. At his trial, Laud was indicted for authorizing the erection of an image of the Blessed Virgin over the new baroque porch of St. Mary's at Oxford. [13] In 1635 Anthony Stafford published, with the approval of the Primate and Bishop Juxon, *The Femall Glory: or, The Life, and Death of our Blessed Lady, the Holy Virgin Mary, God's Owne Immaculate Mother,* one of the most floridly rhetorical productions of the age and one of the most audacious documents of the Anglo-Catholic party. The author addresses his book especially to women: "You who have lived spiritual Amourists, whose spirits have triumphed over the flesh, on whose cheeks Solitude, Prayers, Fasts, and Austerity have left an amiable pale: You who ply your sacred Arithmeticke, and have thoughts colde, and cleane as the christall beads you pray by: You who have vow'd Virginity mentall and corporall. . . . Approach with Comfort, and Kneele downe before the Grand White Immaculate Abbesse of your snowy Nunneries, and presente the All-Saving Babe in her arms, with due Veneration." Stafford gives a long list of the eminent who have "registered their names in the *Sodality* of the *Rosary*

of this our *Blessed Lady*," including Luther and
Calvin; he upholds the Assumption, and he bespeaks
his assurance that he will receive the approbation of
the English Church in affirming that the Virgin was
"a Transcendent Creature, not to be ranked in respect
of her Worth, with any of her sexe, but to have a
place assign'd her apart, and above them all; being
not to be considered as a meere *Woman*, but as a
Type, or an *Idea* of an Accomplished Piety." [14]

Thus the High Anglicans, notably strong at the
universities and among the clergy, sought to revive
pre-Reformation tenets and practices, to establish
their claim to continuity with the ancient church.

Puritan alarm at the rise of the Laudian party was
augmented by the presence, at court, of a French
queen and her retinue and by the natural though un-
just suspicion that the Arminian clergy were Papists in
mask. James' plan for the marriage of his son to the
Spanish Infanta had failed of realization; but in
1625, Charles married Henrietta Maria, daughter of
one Catholic monarch and the sister of another.

The accusations that Laud was an unconfessed
Papist had no truth. At least twice offered a cardi-
nalate if he would submit, he refused.[15] But, on both
the Anglican and the Roman sides, there were sanguine spirits who hoped for reunion; and irenic conferences went on at court. One of the Queen's
chaplains exhibited, though a convert from Anglicanism, a conciliatory desire. Father Sancta Clara had
four or five conversations with Laud, was a favorite

with the King, and published, in 1634, an exposition
of the Thirty-nine Articles, showing them to be susceptible of a Catholic, indeed a Tridentine, interpretation. Three papal agents, Panzani, Con, and Ros-
setti, visited the English court. Panzani entered into
discussions with Bishop Richard Montagu and with
Windebanke, secretary of state. "If . . . we had
neither Jesuits nor Puritans in England," said Windebanke, "I am confident, an union between the
churches might easily be effected." [16]

Until the Civil War, however, conversions to
Rome remained few and chiefly limited to courtiers
and the King's chaplains: such "cases" as those of
Lady Newport and of Walter Montagu, the elegant
son of the very Protestant first Earl of Manchester.
King Charles, reared on the books of Hooker, Andrewes, and Herbert, remained perfectly satisfied
with his sacramental Anglicanism, and, though re-
gardful of his wife's freedom, was eager that his personal attendants should make Anglican communions. [17]

What Catholicly minded Anglicans were most
likely to miss, and to seek outside the national church,
was provision for the contemplative life. England
had—save for Little Gidding, a conventual establishment limited to a single family—no "religious
houses." In developing a devotional literature it was
slow: Cosin's *Devotions*, intended to supply Anglican
gentlewomen with such a manual of private prayers
and acts of devotion as passed current among Catholics, and Stafford's *Femall Glory* attract attention by

their rarity. The devout had chiefly to depend, for
such aids, upon adaptations of pre-Reformation works
like the *Imitatio* and upon such contraband importa-
tions as English versions, printed at Douai or Antwerp
for recusant use, of St. Francis of Sales' *Introduction
à la Vie Dévote* and St. Teresa's autobiography.[18]

In his temperate apologia, published in 1647,
Serenus Cressy, a convert to Rome who became a
Benedictine, made it a chief ground of his defection
from the English Church that it did not provide for
monks and mystics. Anglicans, he says, "renouncing
all Evangelicall Counsills of Perfection, as voluntary
poverty, Charity, etc., and their avarice having swal-
lowed all the revenues which nourished men in a
solitary life of meditation and contemplation, they
both want such effectuall helps thereto, and dare not
for feare of being censured as halfe-Catholiques
command or practise the means proper and conducing
to it, inasmuch as the very name of Contemplation is
unknown among them, I meane in the mysticall
sence. . . ."[19]

For souls who desired an extraordinary piety, even
the Laudians could do little. Their essays at the devotional life seemed timorous and amateurish in comparison with those of the old church. Rome had its
"spiritual directors," under whose tutelage the devout could advance in mental prayer and meditation.
It had its monasteries where the contemplatives might
pass their days in discipline and adoration. It had its
heroes of the Faith, who feared no charge of "en-

thusiasm," confined themselves to no "reasonable
service," but ventured all: those intrepid Jesuits who,
schooled among the sanguinary frescoes of Pomarancio, were tortured and died for the Faith on the
English Mission, in Japan or India, those

> Ripe men of Martyrdom, that could reach down
> With strong arms, their triumphant crown.[20]

Aroused from somnolence by the Reformation,
Rome had, with the Council of Trent (1545–63)
entered upon her own Renaissance. The new order
had its subtractions: the general departure from
the Church of the Scandinavian and Germanic peoples
left her less catholic in temperamental scope; the
presence of doctrinal critics without her borders led
her to renounce much of the speculative freedom per-
missible within an undivided Christendom; there
was a marked impulse to emphasize and exalt whatever tenets, practices, and cults had suffered Protestant opprobrium. But with these retrenchments there
developed a tighter unity, an inflammation of ardor.[21]

The most powerful instrument—almost, indeed,
the symbol—of this Counter-Reformation was the
Society of Jesus, in its foundation almost concurrent
with the Council. Everywhere these martially disciplined, indomitable men took command: in education, in learning, in theology, in the conversion of
Lutherans and infidels, in the creative arts. Themselves ascetic and scrupulously obedient to vicar-gen-
eral and to pope, the Jesuits concealed their iron

hands within softly pliant gauntlets, accommodating themselves, save in matters *de Fide*, to the temperaments and manners of the nations among whom they operated; they sought, Christian humanists that they were, to provide frail human nature with amiable incentives to the practice of religion, and, meanwhile, to set heroic standards for the wills of the spiritually ambitious.

In their astute realism, they saw the importance of controlling education, particularly that of the wellborn; and this purpose they achieved—through their psychological acumen, through their devotion to culture. St. Ignatius, who, while at the College de Sainte-Barbe, had come genuinely to comprehend the spirit of Renaissance humanism, insisted that every novice in his order should, before he began his divine studies, have acquired a knowledge of the humanities. In their academies for the laity, the Jesuits excelled at the teaching of rhetoric and the classics, especially those models of stylistic perfection, Cicero and Vergil; and many became themselves accomplished writers in prose and verse.

Learned Jesuits defended the Church against Protestant criticism, produced works of Biblical, historical, and theological erudition; and other new orders, formed, like the Jesuits, not for monastic seclusion but for offices in the world, testified to the revival of Catholic action.[22]

The chief arguments of the Counter-Reformation were its saints, heroes whose rigor toward themselves

wore, toward others, a persuasive amenity. Though
born to wealth and position, Charles Borromeo,
Archbishop of Milan, founded schools for the poor,
sat by the roadside to teach beggars their *Pater* and
Ave, remained by the sick and dying during the great
plague. Francis Xavier, winning repute for himself
as a professor of philosophy at Paris, became, at the
call of St. Ignatius, a Jesuit, labored for twelve years
in India and Japan, embraced all Asia in his imagination and love, and died as he was about to enter upon
the conquest of China.[23] By his holy sweetness, Philip
Neri, the friend of St. Ignatius, drew to his small
room, affectionately styled the Home of Christian
Mirth, all sorts and conditions of men: the first
families of Rome, Polish nobles, Spanish grandees,
Knights of Malta, archbishops and cardinals, and,
equally, the poor and the ignorant. A mystic, St.
Philip saw, in his visions, the Blessed Virgin; was carried up into Heaven, where his musicianly soul lis-
tened to the choirs of the angelic host; in his old age,
his heart, inflamed by divine love, broke two of his
ribs in its expansion. *Cor meum dilatasti.*[24]

"The saints of the Middle Ages performed miracles; the saints of the Counter-Reformation were
themselves miracles."[25] In Italy, and especially in
Spain, there arose figures whose intellectual power or
practical astuteness or strength of will was accompanied by visions, levitations, trances, raptures, stigmata—states in which the body showed itself incapable of enduring the spiritual passions of its in-

habitant or transparent to them. St. Teresa and St.
John of the Cross, greatest of the Spanish mystics,
attached no decisive importance to these physical
manifestations: those, as they candidly said, might
be pathological, or diabolical, or divine, their test being the effect on the character and the conduct; and
ordinarily, they pointed out, these visions and raptures
disappeared during the culminating mysticism of the
Unitive Way.[26] St. Francis of Sales, fearing that
sanctity might be identified with these spectacular
gifts, asserted: "There are many Saints in heaven who
were never in Extasie, or Rapture of contemplation:
for how many Martyrs, holy men and women, are
mentioned in histories, who never had other privi-
ledge in Praier, than that of devotion and fer-
vour?" [27] But popular piety, ignorant of these warn-
ings, seized upon raptures and stigmata as the marks
of preëminent holiness; and, in the paintings of the
seventeenth century, the great saints of recent times,
like Saints Ignatius, Philip, and Teresa, were nearly
always represented in their moments of vision or rapture.

St. Ignatius and St. Teresa, true Spaniards, united
intense practicality with intense mysticism. Their
natures apprehended vigorously both the world of
the senses and the world which lay within and beyond; yet the outcome was not a dualism of the senses
against the soul. Morally and spiritually they were
dualists: the diabolic principle did not yield in reality
to the divine; metaphors from battle and conflict

came readily to their pens. But the senses, and the imagination which sees in metaphors drawn from the experience of the senses—those they did not distrust. It is precisely in the strong perception of two worlds, the knowledge of men both as they are and as they ought to be, the effort to enlist the imagination in the service of God, that the distinctive character of the Counter-Reformation reveals itself.

CHAPTER TWO

THE MAN

IT WAS under eminently Protestant auspices that Richard Crashaw began his Christian life. Dr. Ussher, professor of divinity at Dublin and later Anglican Primate of Ireland, made triennial visits to England for the purpose of buying books, using the libraries of Oxford, Cambridge, and London, and making the acquaintance of fellow scholars. In 1609, he met the erudite Selden and, in the same year, Selden's friend, the Rev. William Crashaw, active like the Irish scholar in exposing "Romish" forgeries and falsifications. Ussher's next visit to England extended between September, 1612 and April, 1613; and some time during this stay, probably late in 1612, he baptized Crashaw's only son, Richard. Approximately eight years thereafter, October 8, 1620, Ussher preached the funeral of his friend's second wife, and among the many virtues of Elizabeth Crashaw, he notes her "singular motherly affection to the child of her predecessor." [1]

William Crashaw, educated at St. John's College, Cambridge, where he became the disciple of that dominating theologian, William Perkins, held cures of souls in Yorkshire and London: at the time of his son's birth, he was preacher at the Temple Church; at the time of his own death, rector of the then suburban parish of Whitechapel. He was a rigorous Puritan, the enemy of the theater and other worldly pastimes; he hated Popery and the Jesuits. A man of genuine learning and an assiduous collector of books and manuscripts, he was chiefly motivated in his reading and writing by polemic zeal: he desired to expose the superstitious practices of Rome and to establish a continuity between the Faith of Geneva and that of the Church Fathers. Though a purchaser of poetry, he read it for its doctrine alone; and his own verses— translations from the Latin—rarely rise above pious doggerel.[2]

The antithesis between Puritan father and Catholic son is dramatic, and its drama did not escape contemporary notice. Sir Kenelm Digby, writing the Pope in the poet's behalf, calls him "the learned son of a famous Heretic. . . ."[3] About their relation with one another, nothing is to be known; but certainly Richard could scarcely have escaped some acquaintance with his father's library, rich in the literature of Popery. Collected by a Puritan inquisitor though these volumes were, they may well have introduced the poet to Catholic authors and the Catholic spirit. Moreover, the elder Crashaw's persistent, almost hysterical fear of Rome, this Whore of Babylon, this force insidious and menacing, can scarcely have failed to excite the son's concern with the character and claims of a power which, if not diabolic, might indeed be divine.

William Crashaw died in 1626, when his son was but fourteen or thereabouts. Richard was taken under the protection of two lawyers, Sir Henry Yelverton, son of one of William Crashaw's patrons, and Sir Randolph Crew. One of them provided for his board, the other for his clothing till, in 1629, he was furnished both at Charterhouse, where, probably through the mediation of Sir Henry, one of the governors of the school, he was admitted as "gown-boy" or Scholar.[4]

By the will of Thomas Sutton, the governors had established a "hospital" for decayed gentlemen and a school which provided free maintenance and tuition for forty students. The boys thus assisted did not come from the homes of the indigent or the working classes; they were the offspring of knights, baronets, professional men who had no landed estates, persons of breeding and connections who were themselves of very moderate means.[5]

Both hospital and school were housed in the Charterhouse, once a Carthusian monastery, and more recently Howard House, the town mansion of the Duke of Norfolk. Schoolrooms and lodgings for the gown-boys had been adapted from the great building which had served the Duke as tennis court. Accommodations were meager and plain. The boys slept two in a bed; breakfasted and supped on beer, bread,

and cheese; at midday had a dinner of meat, except
on Friday. They dressed in black gowns with white
ruffs.[6]

At Charterhouse, Crashaw came under the tutelage
of Robert Brook, for whose instruction he later, in a
Latin poem, gave affectionate thanks. A strong Royalist, famed for flogging those pupils who did not agree
with him, Brook proved gentle and encouraging to
Crashaw. Under this master, the youth studied the
classical orators and poets, not only construing them
but imitating their style, developing and correcting
his taste by their example.[7]

Concentrating attention upon Greek, Latin, and
rhetoric, the grammar schools of the period afforded
excellent discipline for prospective authors. The practice of double translation, from Latin into English
and back again into Latin, invited the student to
compare his own rhythms, phrasing, and diction with
those of Cicero and Vergil, to the increase of his
taste and discernment; and the transmission of the
substance from verse into prose, prose into verse, and
verse into another meter encouraged flexibility. The
schemes and tropes, as defined by Quintilian, were
taught and practiced. For models and supplies of
exempla, aphorisms, and figurative embellishments,
the students had access to collections like Erasmus'
Adagia and *Similia,* phrase-books like Buchler's
Thesaurus, and anthologies like the *Flores Poetarum,*
which offered elegant specimens of the Latin poets
from Catullus to Ausonius and, for convenience in

use, added an *Index Locorum Communium* listing
nearly three hundred topics. Latin, still the *lingua
franca* of scholars all over Europe, was the medium
of instruction and, by requirement at least, of conversation.[8]

According to the statutes of the founder, the
gown-boys in the highest form were compelled to
write, each Sunday, four Greek and four Latin verses
on some part of the Second or New Testament Lesson for the day. These sacred epigrams, composed
after the fashion introduced into Charterhouse by the
Rev. Sir Robert Dallington, master of Sutton's Hospital, 1624–27, were performed under Brook's super-
vision. Some of the *Epigrammata Sacra* were, perhaps, composed at this period: certainly, Crashaw
acknowledged his former tutor as the *fons et origo*
of that volume.[9]

2. CAMBRIDGE: PEMBROKE

By THE judicious provision of Sutton's will, the boys
of intellectual attainments and promise were, on leaving Charterhouse, given "exhibitions" to the universities. Given such aid, Crashaw matriculated at
Cambridge.[10] On July 6, 1631, he entered Pembroke;
and on October 2 of the same year he was elected a
Greek Scholar upon the Foundation established by
Archdeacon Thomas Watt, an honor earlier held by
the great Lancelot Andrewes. The statutes limit the
candidates to those "of good hope and towardness for

witt and memory, like to continue the course of learning, and well affected toward religion, and the minis-
tery Ecclesiasticall"—that is to say, youths who give
promise of becoming erudite clergy of the English
Church. At the time of their appointment, they must
already be proficient in Latin and Greek grammar,
and competent in Hebrew grammar, must be able to
translate a book of the *Iliad* and the first forty-five
psalms from Apollinarius' edition of the Hebrew.

Those so qualified were provided with a chamber
and a study, with their commons, at tenpence a week,
and with a yearly allowance for their "livery," from
which they were to buy a new gown every alternate
year, and with seven shillings and fivepence a year
for undesignated—but certainly necessary—use.

In return for this subsistence, the Scholars bound
themselves to oratorical and poetic duties. They must
declaim on moral or political *quaestiones* in Latin and
Greek, writing out their essays but delivering them
from memory; and, taking their "argument" from
some passage of scripture appointed for the day, they
must compose four hexameter and four pentameter
Latin verses, and the same number of Greek, for
eleven of the chief holy days of the Church Year, and
two Greek and two Latin verses for every Sunday
and lesser holy day.[11]

Crashaw's college, Pembroke, had been Arminian
in theology and High Church in ritual since the
mastership of Lancelot Andrewes, who was succeeded
by Samuel Harsnett, a man of like temper and views.

The Master of the Hall was now Dr. Benjamin
Laney, vice-chancellor of the University and chaplain
to King Charles. As his sermons published after the
Restoration show, Laney vigorously continued the
tradition of Andrewes. He attacked the Puritans' exaltation of preaching and their fanatical emphasis on
the private conscience; he defended read prayers and
written sermons, the apostolic succession, and the authority of the episcopate. He defined the Anglican
position as "the Faith of God's Word, summ'd up in
the ancient Catholick and Apostolic Forms. . . ."
When, in 1637, Adams, Fellow of Peterhouse,
preached a discourse advocating auricular confession,
and was haled before the Heads on the charge of
heresy, Laney voted for his acquittal.[12]

At his own college, he zealously concerned himself
to restore the ruined and neglected chapel, prescribe
the ritual of the sanctuary and symbolic vestments of
its servitors, and adorn its altar. These pieties won
for him the admiration of the undergraduate poet.[13]

Crashaw's tutor at Pembroke, the Rev. John Tournay, shared the churchmanship of the Master. In
1634 he seriously offended the Puritan party at Cambridge by twice preaching against the doctrine of
Justification by Faith Alone. His pupil's Latin verses
on the same theme, "Fides, quae sola justificat, non est
sine spe et dilectione," may well have been written at
the time of these sensational sermons. Dedicatory
verses show that Crashaw not only respected his tutor,

but that he gained from Tournay encouragement in the pursuit of poetry.[14]

The studies pursued at the Hall were Greek, rhetoric, ethics, logic, and theology. Logic undoubtedly received most attention; with rhetoric it constituted the basis of academic culture. For the development of proficiency in sport and the social arts, the students might receive instruction in tennis, vaulting, dancing, and music.

The chief interest of the Fellows attached to controversial theology and the composition of "commonplaces"—exercises in divinity, delivered in the college chapel. Under Laud's influence, the *Institutes* of Calvin and the works of Perkins and Ames had been supplanted, as theological *summae,* by those of Peter Lombard and St. Thomas Aquinas. A Fellow of Corpus was challenged as disputant at the Commencement of 1631 on the ground that he railed against school divinity, whereas King James, the royal theologian, had commanded that young students in divinity "should apply themselves in the first place to the reading of the Scriptures, next the Councells and ancient Fathers, and then the Schoolmen, excluding those neotericks, both Jesuits and Puritans, who are knowne to be medlers in the matters of State and Monarchy." [15]

The holding of High Anglican views involved, of course, no condonation of papal and Jesuitical iniquities; and, Crashaw, who, from his advent at Pembroke, adopted the theological views of the Laudians, did not immediately lose the anti-Roman hostility implanted in him by his father and as firmly, though less violently, held by most of the Laudians, including Nicholas Ferrar. Three long, posthumously published poems, one beginning

> Grow plumpe, leane Death; his Holinesse a feast
> Hath now praepared . . .

testify to the shudders which the Gunpowder Plot of 1605 could still inspire.[16] And in the preface to his *Epigrammata,* after regretting that the English are so prone to despise their own and prize only what has crossed the Alps, he hints ominously at local Jesuit activity: "let me turn to the acygnian [Ignatian] gentlemen, whom I know . . . to have angrily abandoned me on account of some of my recent sayings. Still, let them compose their temper, and let them confess . . . that they owe me this: that in truth, in so great an argument, they have not recourse to stale untruths concerning their own holy things [*sanctis*] nor to the nauseous calumnies concerning ours." [17] Cambridge Papists had evidently made an attempt to convince Crashaw that Anglican rites were invalid, that true Catholics must be in communion with the See of Peter.

The youth must have brought with him from Charterhouse not only a precocious skill but also some reputation as a poet; for, under the frontispiece of Bishop Andrewes' sermons, the second edition of which was published in 1631, appeared Crashaw's verses, aptly and eloquently hailing the former master of Pembroke and the saintly hero of the young Anglo-Catholics.

In October of the same year, a youthful Fellow of the Hall died, doubtless from the plague then raging in Cambridge; and to the memory of this William Herrys, Crashaw wrote five poems and a Latin epitaph. These may be the expressions of personal emotion; but there was a disparity in their ages and positions, and, though they must certainly have been acquainted, the relation was probably that between Milton and Edward King. Herrys typifies the young man of virtue and attainments prematurely cut off. He may well have been, to Crashaw, an ideal, a hero —this young man whom "Eloquence recognized as an orator; Poetry, as a poet; both as a philosopher; all, as a Christian; who conquered the world by faith, Heaven by hope, his neighbor by brotherly affection, himself by humility; whose mind, under a youthful forehead, was mature; whose austerity of virtue was garbed in ease and grace of manner."

> This is hee in whose rare frame,
> Nature labour'd for a Name,
> And meant to leave his pretious feature,
> The patterne of a perfect Creature.[18]

It was customary at the period for the universities to issue anthologies of Latin verse commemorating all significant events—births, deaths, marriages, and extraordinary providences—in the life of the royal family. During Crashaw's stay at Pembroke, Cambridge assembled such offerings in gratitude for the King's recovery from smallpox (1632), for His Majesty's safe return from a journey to Scotland (1633), and for the birth of the Duke of York (1635). To all three volumes Crashaw contributed. His company boasted academic if not poetic distinction; for, in the first two of these volumes, appeared also Laney, Matthew Wren, Henry More, John Pearson, and Thomas Fuller, Edmund Waller, Thomas Randolph, and Milton's friend, Edward King.[19]

"Amongst his other accomplishments," says the prefacer of *Steps to the Temple*, "hee made his skill in Poetry, Musicke, Drawing, Limming [painting in water-colors and illumination of manuscripts], graving, (exercises of his curious invention and sudden fancy). . . ."

In the couplets, "With a Picture sent to a Friend," [20] probably written while he was at Pembroke, Crashaw self-disparagingly characterized his proficiency at two of his arts:

> I Paint so ill, my peece had need to bee
> Painted againe by some good Poesie.
> I write so ill, my slender Line is scarce
> So much as th' Picture of a well-lim'd
>   verse. . . .

Both preface and couplets imply that his skill at painting equaled that at poetry: such, however, was not the case.

At the time of the erection of the new library at St. John's College, in order to commemorate these benefactions, a handsome manuscript volume, the *Liber Memorialis*, was prepared. Additions to this book long continued to be made; and in July, 1635, Crashaw, still at Pembroke, was commissioned to do three full-page illustrations for it. For the purpose, he copied the portraits, belonging to the College, of King Charles, Archbishop Williams, and Lady Margaret. The colors are still fresh; it cannot, however, be said that the copies show a hand of extraordinary skill: they are the work of an amateur of talent, work suitably styled by Thomas Carre as

> fruites of pure nature; where no art
> Did lead the untaught pensill. . . .

That Crashaw was summoned in from another college might be taken to imply that his graphic talent was generally recognized in Cambridge; but, on the other hand, his father had been a loyal St. John's man, concerned with the enrichment of the new library, and it may well have been this which was primarily responsible for the commission.[21]

To reading and writing, meanwhile, he must chiefly have devoted his care; and, with his fondness for translation and his propensity to seek stimulus for his own imagination in the poetry of others, the two frequently converged. His "literature" in English is difficult to track: though he must have read Spenser, Southwell, Shakespeare, Donne, Ben Jonson, and the Fletchers, he refers only to Sidney, the tragedies of John Ford, and Herbert's *Temple*. The "school" poets—Catullus, Horace, Vergil, and Ovid—he read and reread; and from all save the last he translated; but more characteristic was his taste for the Silver Latinity of Martial, Juvenal, Lucan, Petronius, Claudian, and Ausonius; for the Alexandrian Greek of the *Anthology*, of Heliodorus, of Moschus; and for the Renaissance Latin of John Barclay (from whose *Satyricon* and *Argenis* he translated), of Grotius, of the Jesuits—Strada, Remond, and Hugo.[22] Self-taught in Italian, he paraphrased lyrics from Marino and the Marinists.

In 1634, Crashaw became Bachelor of Arts; and in the same year, he published his *Epigrammata Sacra*, collecting his pious exercises on the Sundays and holy days of the Church Year. Though arranged on no discernible principle, chronological, liturgical, or thematic, the little volume includes three rather regular sequences of Latin epigrams, representing three separate years at Pembroke, and each traversing the sequence of holy days between Christmas and the end of the Epiphany season.[23]

It is likely that all his secular poems were written at Pembroke: some of them, in Latin and on mytho-

logical themes or on ethical commonplaces, may well
be the best of the essays prepared for his tutor in
rhetoric. Most of the poetry was "occasional": in none
is the poet patently autobiographical. Humor absents
his verse, as, undoubtedly, his nature; there appears,
however, in his poem presented "To the Dean on
occasion of sleeping chappell," a kind of substitu-
tionary wit. Love poetry, Latin and Italian, found
him a sympathetic translator; and, in spite of his
ominous meditation on "Thesaurus malorum femina," he had some traffic with young gentlewomen,
to whom, with accompanying gifts of books, he addressed poetic compliments.[24] Significantly, however,
two of the three presentation copies prove to be a
Prayer Book and a copy of *The Temple*.

While still at Pembroke, Crashaw wrote the celebrated "Wishes to his Supposed Mistress," in which
he draws up stipulations for a lady of high character
whose beauty seeks no aid from artifice, whose smiles
warm the blood yet do not threaten chastity. The
mistress is still hypothetical, still to seek; and though,
if she be found, Crashaw confesses himself ready to
capitulate and to unite body as well as spirit, the invitation remained unanswered. Before he left Pembroke, Crashaw had already made his decision.

I would be married, but I'de have no Wife.
I would be married to a single Life— [25]

an intention—if not a vow—which he kept.

3. CAMBRIDGE: PETERHOUSE

THE following year, Crashaw was elected Fellow
of Peterhouse; and, though his formal admission is
dated November 20, 1636, he actually went into
residence a year earlier.[26]

Peterhouse, recollected Colonel Hutchinson, one
of its Puritan graduates, was noted above all the other
colleges in Cambridge for its "Popish superstitious
practices." [27]

During Crashaw's undergraduate years, the Master
of Peterhouse had been Matthew Wren, who had
studied at Pembroke under Andrewes and owed his
early and rapid advancement to the favor of that
great prelate. He attracted the attention of King
James, accompanied Prince Charles on his Spanish
Journey; after leaving Peterhouse, he was, succes-
sively, Bishop of Hereford, of Norwich, and (1638)
of Ely.

At Peterhouse, Wren built a new chapel, consecrated with elaborate ceremonial in 1632, introduced
services in Latin. *Wren's Anatomy*, a Puritan mani-
festo, accused him of attacking sermons and of
adoring the consecrated Host, of "bowing to the
sacrament, and elevating it above his head . . . as
the Priest used to doe in the Masse. . . ." [28]

Elected to the See of Hereford, Wren chose John
Cosin to succeed him at Cambridge. The new master,
formerly canon of Durham, had there achieved a
record to scandalize the Cambridge Puritans. In 1628,

his fellow prebendary, Peter Smart, preached, in the cathedral, an excoriation, attributing to Cosin the inauguration of "altar decking, cope wearing, organ playing, piping and singing, crossing of cushions and kissing of clouts, of starting up and squatting down . . . setting basons on the altar, candlesticks and crucifixes, burning wax candles to excessive number . . . and what is worst of all, gilding of angels and garnishing of images, and setting them aloft." He was further indicted with having called the English reformers "ignorant and unlearned Calvinisticall bishops" and having characterized their Reformation as a Deformation.[29]

To the completion of the small chapel at Peterhouse Cosin gave much attention: he enriched its sanctuary and fostered an "advanced" ceremonial. A marble altar was installed, upon which stood basins, candlesticks, and a celebrated incense-pot, formerly used in the chapel of Bishop Andrewes; over the altar hung a great crucifix. The pavement was marble; the roof was adorned with carved angels; the windows, imported from the Low Countries, were painted glass which it was later to be the relish of the Parliamentarians to destroy. The officiants wore embroidered copes. Thus elegant in its appointments, the chapel appears to have become the center for the Anglo-Catholics of Cambridge. Legends grew up about it. The Scholars from the other houses frequented it, some out of curiosity, some, says Prynne, "to learn and practice the Popish ceremonies and orders used . . . and the common report was that none might approach the altar in Peterhouse but in sandals. . . ." [30]

In the seventeenth century, the colleges still maintained their autonomy. While there were a few ill-attended university lectures, the work of instruction was the responsibility of the college tutors: besides its senior and junior deans and its praelectors, Peterhouse had "readers" in Greek, rhetoric, logic, and ethics, and a catechist. Since the time was one of strong party or sectional feeling, each master sought to impose his views upon those under his authority. Whether he were a North countryman or a South, an Arminian or a Puritan, a Royalist or a Parliamentarian, he gathered about himself young men of his own complexion. To Peterhouse, the Master's influence brought the youth of the great diocese of Durham and the zealots of the High Church party. [31]

Cosin's Peterhouse furnished an atmosphere congenial to Crashaw's mind and temperament. Though his defection to Rome later embittered and estranged the Master, the two men must have been eminently compatible during the period of their association. That Crashaw followed the completion of the chapel with keen interest two impassioned poems remain to demonstrate. [32]

His attitude toward religion, that of the Laudian party, is vigorously expressed in a poem written for prefixion to the *Five Discourses* (1635) of the Rev. Robert Shelford, a venerable alumnus of Peterhouse. The book, which angered and alarmed Archbishop

Ussher, attacks the Puritans and expounds the High Anglican belief and practice.[33] It denies that the Pope is Antichrist; extols good works, liturgical worship, the Sacraments, and the altar; is concerned for the restoration and embellishment of the churches; stresses the "holy vestments" of the clergy, the observance of the "holy feasts," bowing to the altar, fasting communions. Crashaw's poem employs itself specifically on these themes:

> Gods services no longer shall put on
> A *sluttishnesse,* for *pure religion:*
> No longer shall our Churches frighted stones
> Lie scatter'd like the burnt and martyr'd bones
> Of dead Devotion . . .
> No more the hypocrite shall th' *upright* be
> Because he's stiffe, and will confesse no knee:
> While others bend their knee, no more shalt thou,
> (Disdainfull dust and ashes) bend thy brow;
> Nor on Gods Altar cast *two scorching eyes*
> Bak't in hot scorn, for *a burnt sacrifice.* . . .

Faith divorced from works is a mere word, a mere breath of Calvinistic air from Switzerland:

> This shall from hence-forth be the masculine
>   theme
> Pulpits and pennes shall sweat in; to redeem
> Vertue to action, that life-feeding flame
> That keeps Religion warme: not swell *a name*
> Of faith; *a mountaineword,* made up of
>   aire. . . .

With particular vigor, Crashaw denies that hatred of
Rome suffices to make one a good Anglican.

> Nor shall our zealous ones still have a fling
> At that most horrible and horned thing,
> Forsooth the *Pope*. . . .
>   O he is anti-Christ:
> Doubt this, and doubt (say they) that Christ is
>   Christ.
> Why, 'tis a point of Faith. What e're it be,
> I'm sure it is no point of Charitie.
> In summe, no longer shall our people hope,
> To be a true Protestant, 's but to hate the Pope.[34]

But Crashaw, unlike his father, had little taste for
controversy; and he was less concerned to satirize the
Puritans than to discover such "haunts of ancient
peace" and shrines of pious devotion as a troublous
age yet permitted. It is likely that already, in his days
at Pembroke, he had heard of and sought out the
small religious community which had established itself, in the next county of Huntingdonshire, at Little
Gidding.

Its founder, Nicholas Ferrar, was a friend of
George Herbert, who had committed to his care the
manuscript of *The Temple;* and he was himself a
man of marked ability and undoubted sanctity. Born
in 1592, confirmed at the age of six, at seven—in an
agony of prayer and tears—given an assurance of
God's existence and love, later a student at Clare
College, Ferrar was well started on a brilliant career

and had traveled widely when, awakened by a miraculous preservation from an Alpine death, he renounced the world. He was ordained by Laud to the diaconate, beyond which he refused elevation, and retired to Little Gidding, where his mother had purchased a ruined mansion. Here he established, in 1626, what may be fairly called the first "religious" house after the Reformation. The conventual family comprised Ferrar, his aged mother, his middle-aged brother and brother-in-law, and their children. They restored the manor house; returned the chapel, which had fallen into use as a haybarn, to its sacred uses. They established a system of daily offices, one for each hour, consisting of Psalms, a portion of the Gospel, and a hymn; three times a day, the family visited the church, going in order, two by two. After the monastic custom, the meals were silent, the place of conversation being taken by the reading aloud from the Bible, Foxe's *Book of Martyrs*, volumes of history and travel.[35]

To these day offices, Ferrar, at the suggestion of his friend, George Herbert, added a nightly vigil, kept from nine till one; either two men or two women, in their own oratory, knelt and recited the whole Psalter. After his mother's death, Nicholas Ferrar slept upon a bearskin on the floor; he watched either in the oratory or in the church, three nights in the week; and on the nights when he slept, he rose at one and spent the rest of the night in prayer and meditation.

The contemplative life did not exclude the practical, for the community busied themselves with appropriate works of charity and devotional use. They established a school where their own children, and those of the neighboring gentry, might learn penmanship, grammar, arithmetic, Latin, and music, as well as virtue. On Sundays Ferrar's nieces conducted a class for the poor children of the surrounding parishes; and, having been instructed by their uncle in the dressing of wounds and preparation of salves, they visited the poor and sick in their homes.

Ferrar's brother-in-law, Collett, begot sixteen children, chiefly girls. All were taught embroidery and music and fine penmanship and bookbinding. They excelled at a special handiwork, the manufacture of what were variously called Harmonies or Concordances, richly bound volumes offering the texts of the Four Gospels arranged in one continuous history, and illustrated with fine Continental engravings. At His Majesty's request, one was made for King Charles, who twice visited the community at Little Gidding, and held it in high respect.[36]

Mary Collett, the eldest of Ferrar's nieces, and her sister Anna, two years her junior, dedicated themselves to celibacy; and, though Bishop Williams refused to sanction their adoption of vows and the virgin's veil, they persisted faithful to their private resolution.[37]

Like the chapel at Peterhouse, Little Gidding attracted sundry classes of visitors. The hostile came to spy upon and revile the "Arminian Nunnery";

the idle and curious, to amuse themselves with this much-bruited innovation. But there came also, says Isaak Walton, "many of the clergy that were more inclined to practical piety and devotion than to doubtful and needless disputation."[38]

Among these pious pilgrims was Crashaw, who grew to be an intimate of the family, rejoiced in their way of life, and frequently rode over from Cambridge to pass his days in the ordered sequences of the offices and to share in the night watches. In his free translation from Barclay's *Argenis*, the "Description of a Religious House and Condition of Life," he was assuredly commemorating Little Gidding.[39]

> Obedient slumbers that can wake and weep,
> And sing, and sigh, and work, and sleep again;
> Still rowling a round sphear of still-returning
>   pain.
> Hands full of harty labours; Paines that pay
> And prize themselves; doe much, that more they
>   may,
> And work for work, not wages. . . .
> No cruell guard of diligent cares, that keep
> Crown'd woes awake; as things too wise for
>   sleep.
> But reverent discipline, and religious fear,
> And soft obedience, find sweet biding here;
> Silence, and sacred rest; peace, and pure joyes;
> Kind loves keep house, ly close, and make no
>   noise,

And room enough for Monarchs, while none
  swells
Beyond the kingdomes of contentfull Cells.

Ferrar Collett, nephew of Little Gidding's founder
and head, became one of Crashaw's few pupils at
Peterhouse.[40]

Queen Elizabeth and her ministers designed both
universities to serve primarily as training schools for
an educated and patriotic clergy; and, till the last
quarter of the nineteenth century, it continued to be
the requirement that the Fellows should be celibate
during their tenure of office and that they should
either be in Holy Orders or in preparation to receive
them. With this requirement, Crashaw's personal
desires were, of course, in perfect accord.[41]

Of his entrance into Holy Order, no record exists;
but priest he certainly was by 1639, for in that year
he held the curacy of Little St. Mary's, formerly the
chapel of Peterhouse as well as parish church.[42]
Even after the erection of Wren's new chapel, in
1632, the connection between college and church remained close. The living was in the bestowal of the
College; contributions were made to the stipend
of the curate; and a second story passageway joined
the gallery of the Church to the rooms of the College,
the nearest chamber generally belonging to the Fellow in charge. Crashaw presumably continued his
curacy from the late spring of 1639 till his departure
from Cambridge in January, 1643.

In the later years of his fellowship, he held office also at Peterhouse, as its catechist.

As a method of instructing children and uneducated adults, catechizing was a party issue of the day. The Laudians practiced and defended it as a form of objective and systematic religious teaching, while the Puritans attacked it and substituted sermons and "lectures." The college catechist, however, had a different function than had the parish priest. Perkins, whose works were edited by Crashaw's father, held the office at Christ's; Lancelot Andrewes, at Pembroke. As catechist, Andrewes instituted a series of Saturday and Sunday afternoon lectures on theology and ethics, lectures thronged with hearers—distinguished members of the University and young priests from the country parishes. The college catechist was in effect a theological tutor or lecturer.

Both as a catechist and as curate, Crashaw must have preached: it is a matter for regret that none of his discourses survives. A seventeenth-century biographer, Lloyd, describes Crashaw's "thronged sermons on each Sunday and Holiday, that ravished more like Poems . . . scattering not so much Sentences as Exstasies; his soul breathing in each word. . . ." Poetic and ecstatic discourses: these are surely the sort Crashaw must have preached.

If his sermons were at once so eloquent and so popular, why have they not, like those of Andrewes and Donne, come down to us? One may conjecture that Crashaw himself had care only for his reputa-

tion as a poet, and destroyed his sermons before he
left Cambridge; or that they fell into the hands of
the intruded Puritan Fellows and by them were given
to the flames; or that the sermons were extemporized.

For the nature of his homiletic exegesis, the
Epigrammata may fairly be taken as an indication.
Most of them found their inspiration in the Gospels
and Epistles of the Prayer Book, and from these same
Gospels and Epistles Crashaw must, according to
Anglican use, customarily have preached.

Crashaw's life at Cambridge appears to have been
modeled on that of the community at Little Gidding.
He observed " a rare moderation in diet," was sparing
in his use of wine. So far as possible, he passed his
time in Little St. Mary's, often spending the night
in "watching" and prayer, and there he is said to have
composed his poems.[43]

Seventeenth-century Cambridge might fairly avow
itself England's Helicon. Giles Fletcher, Donne,
George Herbert, Thomas Randolph, Marvell, Suckling, and Cowley were all Trinity men. Phineas
Fletcher was of King's; Benlowes (about ten years
Crashaw's senior) was of St. John's; Joseph Beaumont was of Peterhouse. Milton was at Christ's till
1632. John Cleveland, almost exactly Crashaw's contemporary, was Fellow of St. John's from 1634 till
1642.

Of these poets, Cowley and Beaumont became
Crashaw's intimates. The former, a child prodigy, had
already published two books of verse before 1637,

when he came to Trinity. In the same year, a third edition of *Poetical Blossoms*, published when its author was fifteen, appeared from the press of Henry Seile; and there can be little doubt that "Upon two green apricots sent to Cowley by Sir Crashaw" is a graceful acknowledgment of this third edition. Allusion to the book's title appears in the following lines, along with poetic exaggeration of the poets' disparity in years—only five.

> O had my wishes,
> And the deare merits of your Muse, their due,
> The yeare had found some fruit early as you;
> Ripe as *those rich composures time computes*
> *Blossoms*, but our blest tast confesses fruits.
> . . . .
> How then must these,
> Poore fruites looke pale at thy Hesperides!
> Fain would I chide their slownesse, but in their
> Defects I draw mine owne dull character.
> Take them, and me in them acknowledging,
> How much my summer waites upon thy spring.[44]

At Peterhouse, Crashaw acquired the companionship of Joseph Beaumont, four years his junior, who became Fellow in 1636. This friend, in comprehensive accord with Crashaw's tastes, was a royalist, a churchman of "advanced" sympathies, a painter, and a poet; he read Hebrew, Greek, Latin, Italian, Spanish, and French. In the course of a Latin oration delivered in 1638, and ambitiously surveying the whole range of the humane studies, Beaumont exhibited a wide knowledge of poetry and a catholicity in his poetic enthusiasms: Tasso, Marino, Sannazaro, du Bartas, Ronsard. An ecstatic paragraph introduced, to the Anglicans of Cambridge, the name of the Spanish mystic, Teresa of Avila: "I see her whose pen, wet with divine dew, dripped I know not what sweeter than sweetness itself, and bathed the whole heaven. Do you await the name of the heroine? It is Saint TERESA, a name unheard by you, I believe, and more familiar to angels than to our men. O with what sweetness may you breathe your last in her writing! O how least a death would it be, in her writings to die!" [45]

Beaumont studied the Schoolmen. He venerated the saints, compiling, for his private devotions, a calendar in which the lives of these Christian heroes were arranged, after the fashion of Catholic *Vitae Sanctorum,* under their feast days. In defense of post-Biblical and post-Apostolic miracles, he wrote a Latin dissertation which exposed him, in the judgment of his latter-day editor, to grave suspicion of credulity. [46] He attached high importance to virginity, and, whether or not he made a vow, did not marry till after six years of struggle to remain celibate. He reverenced the Church, orthodoxy, antiquity, the priesthood, the Holy Sacrament.

Beaumont's poetry, chiefly religious, commemorated the holy days of the Christian year, celebrating, among the saints, not merely the neutral apostles but such un-Anglican figures as St. Joseph, St. Gregory of Nazianzen, and even St. Simon Stylites.[47] His *Psyche,* published in 1652, is a vast allegory of twenty cantos, obviously based upon much spiritual reading in the French and Spanish masters: it attempts to poetize the whole chronicle of the mystical life, its alternative aridities and refreshments, its temptations and tortures, its trances and ecstasies, the Dark Night of the Soul, and its final union with God. In style, it combines Spenser and the Fletchers with a copious and overpowering draft from Crashaw. Beaumont is frequently naïve, almost always prolix; along with much genuine but diffused and sentimental emotion, he seems incited by his reading of spirits more intense than his own and, probably, by his association with Crashaw, to work himself into factitious raptures; in consequence of this his Marinistic style—his antitheses, paradoxes, oxymorons, and conceits—seems sometimes to be a mere ritual, learned by rote and perpetuated without thought. All of his shorter poems, as well as his allegorical "epic," belong to the period after both poets had left Cambridge; but Crashaw's influence dominates them. In one passage of the *Psyche,* ample enough to allow of many digressions, Beaumont passes in review the bards, praising as lyric poets Pindar, Horace, and George Herbert, as epic poets, Homer, Vergil, Tasso, and Spenser. A eulogy of St. Gregory Nazianzus, the fourth-century poet of the Eastern Church, then introduces two stanzas on

Crashaw, without whom he is "half-lost," who is his "only worthy Self." [48]

4. EXILE: LEYDEN, PARIS

A SERENELY happy life this: a fellowship in a college strongly Anglo-Catholic; a curacy in Little St. Mary's; frequent retreat to Little Gidding.

This life was now to be disrupted. After years of verbal combat between Royalist and Puritan, Calvinist and Arminian, the controversy took arms. There arrived, in June, 1642, a royal letter, summoning Cambridge contributions to the King's defense against Parliament. Among the compliant colleges, Peterhouse lent sixty pounds—Crashaw, among other Fellows, signing his name to the guarantee. [49] By way of revenge, the townsmen, chiefly Parliamentary in their sympathies, fired at the windows of some collegians.

In the spring of 1643, Cromwell seized Cambridge, occupying it with an army of nearly thirty thousand, later reduced to a permanent garrison of a thousand. In December of the same year, the Parliamentary Commissioners, working under an act empowering the demolition of superstitious and idolatrous monuments, visited Peterhouse, where they tore down the carved angels and the statues of the Four Evangelists and of St. Peter. At Little St. Mary's, they found and destroyed "sixty Superstitious Pictures, Some Popes and Crucifixes and God

the father sitting in a chayer. . . ." [50] Meanwhile,
during the year, the soldiers quartered in the town
assisted in the purgation, demolishing all carved work
in the chapels, burning the furniture of the Fellows'
chambers, felling collegiate orchards and groves. Out
of the plunder drawn from the Fellows' rooms, the
soldiers reserved the religious pictures, "Popish
Idols" of the University, making of them, in the
market place, a holocaust; the consequence was to
inflame the commoner sort of townspeople till "a
Scholar could have small security from being stoned
or affronted as he walked the streets." [51]

From witnessing this profanation of things dear,
Crashaw was spared. Not formally ejected from his
fellowship till June, 1644, he left Peterhouse in the
latter part of January.[52]

Behind him remained his friend and former pupil,
Ferrar Collett, now a By-Fellow; and on March 12,
Collett received for Crashaw certain disbursements
made in payment for the latter's services as catechist
at Somersham, Colne, and Pidley.[53]

The exile first retired, it is likely, to Little Gidding.
In February, 1644, however, he was in Leyden,
whence he wrote to one of the Ferrars. He has experienced estrangement from Mary Collett, who, since
1632, had been the "Mother" of the community in
Huntingdonshire, and is throughout the letter re-
ferred to by her title; or, rather, she is not allowed
to see him by her uncles, in whose home at Leyden
she is staying. It may well have been that Crashaw

was already headed Romeward, and that for such treason Miss Collett's Protestant relatives forbade him their house. Whatever the objection, his feeling about her is still unchanged. She is still "the gentlest kindest most tender-hearted and liberall handed soul. . . ." [54]

He encloses a resignation of his fellowship in behalf of Ferrar Collett, hoping that his correspondent and Joseph Beaumont will together be able to effect this transfer, and that, unlikely as it seems, he himself may one day return to Cambridge. "I have I assure you no desire to be absolutely and irrespectively rid of my beloved Patrimony in St. Peter. No man than myself holds more high the humble scepter of such a little contentfull kingdom. And as safely may I say no man more unprovided of any present course."

Separated from Peterhouse and now from Mary Collett, what course can Crashaw take? What, save resignation to God? "His good pleasure his gratious providence, the one for the end, the other for the way meanes to it, into these do I desire to resolve my totall self." But the whole effect of his misfortunes has been comparable to a concussion: put into temporal and spiritual exigence, he feels wrenched, bewildered. Yet the workers of his persecution—surely they have used him but as a poor sinner deserves and, through their malice, have been the instruments of God's will and design.

As for the present, which he is too weak to confront

manfully: he is at Leyden, and finds its atmosphere
totally alien to his spiritual peace. The people are
given over to idolatry—to the worship of wealth and
secular learning. From their great church they have
removed a window filled with saints in order to install
Minerva—spear, helmet, owl, and all. Either "not
scholler enough or not Pagan enough for this place,"
he must leave this Athens of Holland and resume
his travels.

A sentence shows that he had for some time been
purposing a radical decision, and that Ferrar had
begged him to delay it. This, he writes, he has done;
but, though it will please his counselor, he himself
judges it rather a fault that he has not yet been able
to fix his "weak soul to severer courses."

What decision was he delaying to make? Submission to Rome, one must suppose. The motives for
his hesitance were strong. A change of church would
prohibit all hope of return to his beloved patrimony
at Peterhouse. Further, his intimates, the Ferrars,
Beaumont, and Dr. Cosin were, for all their Catholic
devotions, equally staunch opponents of "Popery,"
and remained loyal to their Anglican heritage
through the twenty years when its recovery seemed
a lost cause. It was altogether probable that this
projected move might lose him his friends.

What persuaded him to his decision? Not dissatis-
faction with Anglican theology as expounded by
Laud and Montagu, as preached by Andrewes and
Donne, as illustrated by the poetry of George

Herbert. Not dissatisfaction with Anglican ceremonial as practiced at Peterhouse, nor with the
Anglican "religious life" as exemplified by Little
Gidding. Crashaw's so-called "Apologie" contains
no repudiation of Anglicanism; still more striking,
one can search in vain through the "Letter to the
Countess of Denbigh," penned to hasten her surrender to Rome, without finding any hint, much less
explicit statement, of Roman claims, or any answer
to Anglican objections.[55]

Had the Civil War not rudely terminated an
epoch, Crashaw would probably have died an Anglican. Indeed, during the troubled remainder of his
life, he must sometimes have indulged in such sentimental retrospect of his life in the age of Laud and
Charles as visited his friend, Joseph Beaumont, when,
after the Restoration, he apostrophized the Martyr
King: "And was not the Land most blessed in him?
In civil respects; was it not the Paradise where Peace,
Plenty, and Honor, securely flourished, whilst they
were nipped and blasted in other Nations? Was not
this the Object of the World's Envy, and yet so
secured, as that all Envy could not indanger it? In
ecclesiastical respects: was it not the onely Sanctuary
of the truely Catholik and Apostolic Faith and Discipline? Was not God's Service amongst us happily
protected from Superstition on one hand, and from
Profanes on the other? . . . Join both respects together, and were not the forged prerogatives of the

Golden Age, I say, not copied, but really transcended, by our felicity . . . ?" [56]

But to Crashaw this Golden Age seemed over and gone. He came to hold, says Anthony à Wood, an "infallible foresight that the Church of *England* would be quite ruined by the unlimited fury of the Presbyterians." [57] And there was nothing in the nature of his faith to deter his conversion. The obstacles were personal: the possible severance of relations with his friends. The incentive was strong. Unlike his father, he did not relish combat: he craved peace.

In the Catholic Church Crashaw could find all which had been dear to him in the Anglican, and find it accepted as, beyond dispute, valid and valuable. Cosin's *Devotions*, reverence done the altar, Little Gidding—all the brave little attempts at manuals of piety, ceremonial, and the monastic life which, in the English Church, encountered suspicion and persecution, could, at Rome, be had without effort; and, where Anglicanism could point to a devout Lancelot Andrewes, a "judicious Hooker," and a "holy George Herbert," a Charles and a Laud martyred for their loyalty to apostolic faith and order, the Communion of Rome could display saints and martyrs without number.

That Crashaw returned from Leyden to England seems probable; and, since the King's court was in residence at Oxford from July, 1643 to April, 1644, it is also probable that Crashaw took refuge at the last stronghold of the Royalist cause. According to hearsay, Crashaw had been incorporated at Oxford in 1641; and more reliable testimony, a letter from the Queen, reports Crashaw a member of both universities.[58] Perhaps it was at Oxford that he made his submission to Rome, which appears to have occurred in 1645, shortly before his final departure from England.

In 1645 he took up residence in Paris, where Queen Henrietta Maria had established her court a year before. Loyally, she served as patroness of the Royalist exiles, in particular those of her own faith. Her chief favorites were such Catholic priests as Walter Montagu, Thomas Vane, Hugh Cressy, Thomas Carre, and Stephen Goffe—all men of high culture; all, save one, converts.[59]

Goffe, like Crashaw the son of a Puritan divine, had been, as Anglican, chaplain to King Charles, and Royalist agent in France, Flanders, and Holland. After the King's cause had been lost, he retired to France, made his submission to Rome, and entered the French Oratory, rising, in 1655, to be the superior. He generously used both his means and his influence in behalf of the English exiles, Protestant as well as Catholic—among them, it is said, Cowley.[60]

Carre, apparently born Catholic, had lived abroad all his life. At Douai, till 1634, he was procurator of the famous college established to educate English Catholics. Later, at Paris, he founded Mount St.

Sion, a convent of Augustinian canonesses; and till his death he served as confessor to this community of English emigrées. Held in high esteem by the court of France, especially by Cardinal Richelieu, he was, like Goffe, a preëminent patron of exiled English Catholics.[61]

Those attached to the Stuart court were not all of the Queen's faith. Though Dr. Cosin's own son and four Fellows of Peterhouse had made their submission to Rome, the ejected master, who served as chaplain to the Anglican exiles at Paris, stood firm. In 1646, he wrote bitterly to a friend, "of Mr. *Crashaw,* etc. I know too much, but I am more glad to hear you say, that you have no thought of following their ungracious and fond fancies. God ever preserve you and me in our old way of Truth; from which no Persecution shall ever drive us." [62] And Abraham Cowley, Anglican diplomat and poet, spent ten years in the Queen's circle and in her service.

Hearing that Crashaw was in Paris, Cowley sought him out; and when he found his friend in a state of destitution, he shared with him his own slender means. Hereafter Crashaw, probably through Cowley's introduction, met Goffe and Carre, and through them the Queen.[63]

Crashaw had all his life been a devout Royalist, faithfully celebrating in verse the coronation of King Charles, all important and some unimportant events in his career, and he had hailed the successive births of the Stuart progeny; but to Henrietta Maria, pious Catholic and protector of the faithful, he must now have felt a special allegiance. In common they had the cult of the great St. Teresa, for whom the Queen felt a strong devotion. To Her Majesty, Crashaw inscribed his "Glorious Epiphany," presenting it to her at Twelfth-night.[64]

With the Queen in Paris was her lady in waiting, Susan Villiers, Countess of Denbigh. The sister of the Duke of Buckingham, she was a woman of piety; but—like her mother, for whose continuance in the Anglican faith Laud conducted his conferences with Fisher, and like her daughter, Lady Kynalmeaky, who turned Papist, reverted to the Church of England, and finally became Catholic for the rest of her life—the Countess was unstable in her ecclesiastical allegiance. She was among the great ladies of the court who accepted sacred pictures, relics, and medals from the Pope's agents, Panzani and Con. For her edification, Cosin compiled his *Devotions;* and it was probably due to his vigilance and controversial skill that she was still, in 1645, a communicant of the English Church.[65]

It is possible that Crashaw had been presented to the Countess when, between 1643 and 1644, the King's court held residence at Oxford; but however they met, this "noblest and best of ladies," as Crashaw calls her, became his patroness. *Carmen Deo Nostro,* published in 1652, three years after his death, is dedicated to her, "in hearty acknowledgment of his immortal obligation to her goodness and charity." And the inaugural poem is an address to the Countess, warning her against "irresolution and delay in matters of religion" and bidding her to "render herself without further delay into the communion of the Catholic church." This counsel, the best return his impoverished self could offer her generosity, was not taken during the poet's lifetime. The Countess still hesitated, still delayed, till the Easter of 1651, when she finally made her submission. A year later she died, "with all the marks of a predestined soul," and was buried in the fashionable Church of St. Eustache.[66]

With Carre, Crashaw formed a close friendship:

Yes, Car's Crashawe, he Car; t'is love alone
Which melts two harts, of both composing one.

The chaplain of the Augustinian canonesses delighted in books, wrote poetry, possessed skill at painting, at copper engraving, at sculpture.[67] Like Crashaw's, his temperament was devotional and mystical rather than polemic. He translated into English St. Francis of Sales' *Treatise of the Love of God,* two books by the Salesian, Camus, four books attributed to Thomas à Kempis. His original work, *Pietas Parisiensis,* is an apologetic for Rome based upon the superior ardor of Catholic devotional life.

Carre has described his friend as he knew him in Paris, admired by the "strongest wits," loved by all, impervious to his surroundings, dead to self.

> . . . heavenly riches . . . wholy call'd
> His thoughtes from earth, to live above in th'
>   aire
> A very bird of paradice. No care
> Had he of earthly trashe.
>
> . . . .
>
> . . . to him one God is all; all's one.
> What he might eate or weare he tooke no
>   thought;
> His needfull foode he rather found than sought.
> He seekes no downes, no sheetes, his bed's still
>   made.
> If he can find a chaire or stoole, he's lay'd;
> When day peepes in, he quitts his restless rest,
> And still, poore soule, before he's up he's
>   dres't.[68]

Thus he lived an ascetic life, continuing and intensifying the regimen he had first known at Little Gidding.

But he was impelled to move on to Italy; and in September, 1646, the Queen wrote in his behalf to the Pope: "Mr. Crashaw, having been a Minister in England and nourished in the Universities of this country among people very remote from the senti-

ments of our Holy Religion, has nevertheless by his
Reading and his study become a Catholic and, to en-
joy more peaceably the exercise of his religion, has
transported himself hence, and has dwelt nearly a
year near me, where by the good example of his life
he has greatly edified all who have conversed with
him: Which has incited me at his going to Rome to
write this word to your Holiness to pray you to consider him as a person of whom the English Catholics
have conceived great hopes, and whom I much
esteem, and to bestow upon him graces and favors as
occasion may present." [69]

5. ITALY: ROME, LORETO

CRASHAW set out for Rome, and lingered there for
a year without receiving aid or attention. Had he
arrived in the preceding pontificate, he might have
fared better, for Urban VIII, a great prince of the
Barberini family, was the fosterer of painters and
poets as well as fortifications; he had himself published sacred verse, turning the scriptural canticles
into Horatian and Sapphic meters. But Innocent X,
who succeeded him in 1644, was a man of another
stamp, austere and markedly less the Maecenas. [70]

The Queen wrote again in behalf of the "learned
son of a famous heretic," reminding Innocent that in
a year's time, "tho' assaulted on the one hand by
many grievous and dangerous infirmities, and on

the other hand with extreme want and necessities," Crashaw had found no assistance from His Holiness.[71]

This request appears to have been heeded; for when John Bargrave, till his ejection Fellow of Peterhouse, visited Rome in 1646–47, he found Crashaw in the service of Cardinal Pallotta. Each ecclesiastical prince had his *Sequita,* or corps of scantily paid gentlemen, who, elaborately trained in the etiquette of the papal court, added pomp to the ceremonial movements of their masters.

Held in high esteem by the Pope, the hierarchy, and the citizens of Rome, Cardinal Pallotta was "a man of an angelical life." He exhibited courage by warning Innocent that the autocratic rule of his sister-in-law, Donna Olympia, had shocked the city. Affable and urbane, he was also a man of deep piety. Crashaw found in him a prelate whose holiness justified his office.[72]

The Cardinal's retinue felt, however, no obligation to follow their master's way of life. Crashaw, disgusted by their "wickedness," reported it to Pallotta. The other attendants, Italians, must have resented the presence of an Englishman, even had he not been a man of Crashaw's ascetic discipline; and his talebearing aroused their hot blood. In concern for Crashaw's safety, the Cardinal, in 1649, appointed him to a minor post, that of *beneficiatus,* at Loreto.[73]

Here Crashaw was to pass the last months of his

life. Loreto, a popular resort for pilgrims since the fifteenth century, possessed one of the most sacred shrines in Christendom. According to tradition, it was in the *Santa Casa* that the Blessed Virgin had been born, had heard the Annunciation of the Angel Gabriel, had conceived the Son of God, and had lived with St. Joseph and her Divine Child. In the thirteenth century, eight days before the Saracens' capture of Acre ended Christian rule in Palestine, this Holy House suddenly disappeared. Transported through the skies by angels, it reached the Italian village of Tersato in 1291; three years later, the angels moved it again; and thrice, till at last it took its permanent rest at Loreto. A tiny house of stone, resting on no foundations, it was necessary to shelter it from injury and profanation and to make possible the reception of pilgrims. In 1350, the first church was erected about the *Santa Casa;* in 1468, the present great basilica succeeded to it; in 1531, the outer walls of the Casa were encrusted with marble adorned in bas-relief. Pious opinion has it that the original altar was consecrated by St. Peter, that the crucifix was placed there by the Apostles, and that St. Luke carved the statue of the Blessed Virgin.[74]

St. Francis Xavier twice visited Loreto. St. Charles Borromeo traveled thither on foot, fifty miles. St. Stanislaus Kostka, praying there, felt such inflamed devotion that afterwards, even in winter, he often found it necessary to cool his heart with freezing water. St. Francis of Sales, having journeyed on

foot from Rome, kissed the walls of the Holy
House.[75]

The marbles, the frescoes, the images, the blazing
candles and lamps; the *Santa Casa* itself, where
dwelt the Mother of God and the Word made Flesh;
the shrine enriched by the pilgrimages of the multi-
tudes and the Saints: one can conjecture the bliss
which must have been Crashaw's during the final
few months of his life. He was inducted into his office
on the twenty-fourth of April, 1649. The "holy
ardor of his soul overheating his body," he died on
the twenty-first of August, and was buried "in
tumulo sacerdotum." [76]

Upon hearing of his death, his friend Cowley,
though an Anglican, hailed the end as appropriate
and the life as that of a saint.

How well (blest swan) did Fate contrive thy
    Death,
And made thee render up thy tuneful Breath
In thy great *Mistress* Arms? Thou most Divine
And richest *Off'ring* of *Loretto's Shrine!*
Where like some holy *Sacrifice* t'expire,
A *Fever* burns thee, and *Love* lights the *Fire.*
Angels (they say) brought the fam'd *Chappel*
    there,
And bore the sacred Load in Triumph thro' the
    Air.
'Tis surer much they brought *thee* there, and
    they,

And *thou,* their Charge, went *singing* all the
way. . . .
Poet and *Saint!* to thee alone are giv'n
The two most sacred *Names* of *Earth* and
Heav'n. . . ."[77]

Crashaw, says Anthony à Wood, was a "mere
scholar, and shiftless," a pair of epithets which we
may translate into "bookish and impractical." The
pattern of his career corroborates this estimate of his
outer aspect. His real life, the inner life of sensibility
and contemplation in which habitually he dwelt,
could not present public exhibition, but it has revealed
itself in his poetry.[78]

The lineaments of his nature thus descried are,
though hardly normal, not complex. Two interests,
the arts and religion, dominated his whole life. In
both, he found his way, without apparent struggle,
toward the goal predestined by his temperament.

Like his Philomela, Crashaw was "music's En-
thusiast." Apt at languages and conversant with four
literatures, he showed no taste for speculation and
little for self-analysis. He never reasons in his poems
or in his prefaces; evinces, save for a few Platonic
and Neo-Platonic allusions, no knowledge of meta-
physics, whether of the Greeks or of the moderns;
does not concern himself with ecclesiastical arguments.

Sensuous rather than intellectual, he might have
proved voluptuary, libertine, or aesthete; and, de-

voted to the cause of beautifying college chapels and elaborating their ceremonials, he might be set down as a ritualist. Yet such he clearly was not. The rigor of his boyhood Puritanism, the sojourns at Little Gidding, his reading in hagiography—something turned him into the way of the ascetic. He eschewed wine, fasted, spent his nights in prayer, lived—both at Cambridge and at Paris—like an anchorite.

Unlike his great contemporary, Milton, he was gentle and docile of nature; during his career in school and university, he felt sincere respect and affection for those set over him; his poems to Brook, Tournay, and Laney bespeak more than the conventional flattery bestowed upon a patron; his self-distrust, his desire for corroboration, his *minimus tuorum* all appear quite unaffected.

His strongest personal attachments, both actual and imaginative, bound him to women—his kind stepmother, Mary Collett, the Countess of Denbigh, the Queen, St. Teresa, the Queen of Heaven.

His was a flaming heart: salamander-like, he lived in fire as his natural element; desiring a commonplace and orderly existence, he placed his happiness in essential ecstasy. Some of the secular poems attain untroubled rapture; in the religious poems, it is sometimes the joy three-fourths pain.

A sensuous nature, coupled with an ardent devotion to unseen realities: the two become approximately fused in the spiritual atmosphere and in the aesthetic of the Counter-Reformation.

CHAPTER THREE

INTERLUDE: BAROQUE ART AND THE EMBLEM

TRIDENTINE Catholicism found graphic and plastic embodiment in the painting of Correggio, Murillo, El Greco, Rembrandt, Rubens, Guido Reni, and the Carracci, in the sculptures of Bernini, in the emblem books of the Jesuits and Benedictines; it transformed Rome into a city of magnificent churches, where the *Seicento* still lingers.

Here, in this pictorial world, will be found, urged with sensual power, all the themes which compelled the baroque imagination: angels and cherubs, the Infant Jesus, the shepherds and kings doing homage to the Nativity, the Circumcision, the crucified Saviour from whose wounds flow water and blood, the Sacred Heart, the Pietà, *quem transivit gladius*, the Assumption of the *Mater Dei*, the weeping Magdalen, the ecstatic Teresa, the Holy Innocents, the ripe men of martyrdom, the mystics receiving the stigmata or swooning in trances or carried into the seventh heaven, hearing the music of the angels, and, finally, the Day of Judgment when this miraculous globe dissolves into ashes and the trumpet of doom, *mirum spargens sonum*, calls the souls to final separation.[1]

In the painting of the Counter-Reformation, under the close surveillance of theologians, who assigned the artists their subjects, and, in considerable measure, prescribed the treatment,[2] lie incarnate the religious life of the age, its attitudes and its themes. Everywhere in Italian churches one sees depicted the new devotions—the angels, who float rosily among the clouds of Jesuit frescoes; the Holy Family; St. Joseph; the Infant Jesus, devotion particularly dear to the cloister. Traditional themes assume untraditional treatment. The uncovering of the Catacombs and the missionary deaths in India, South America, and Protestant Europe magnified the cult of martyrdom; but, whereas, in the Middle Ages, the martyrs had been depicted triumphant of countenance, they were now represented writhing in the agony of torture or enduring ingeniously cruel death; they struggle before our eyes, roasting in flames or streaming with blood.[3] Under the influence of Bernini, whose statue of Alexander VII was immediately felt to be a master work, the skeleton became a familiar equipage of mortuary monuments, while the tense and sometimes agitated effigies of the dead seem remote from the serene sleep with which the thirteenth century endowed them.[4] The saints, ordinarily visualized by medieval art in the performance of miracles, now appear as recipients of miraculous grace; and the composure of their faces and figures, the tranquil amenity of Raphael's Virgins, has yielded to the physically contorted pattern of the trance or the rapture.[5] The contraventions of law and reason which Protestantism sought to minimize are everywhere selected for celebration. Common sense and sober judgment, the "wisdom of this world," are flagrantly violated; and prudence is made to seem a paltry thing in comparison to the extremes, often united, of pain and ecstasy.

The baroque style is exuberant, rhetorical, sensual, grandiose. The repose and symmetry of Renaissance art have yielded to agitation, aspiration, ambition, an intense striving to transcend the limits of each genre. Sculpture and architecture would elicit the effects of painting; painting—weary of exact draftsmanship, clearly outlined masses, grouping within the plane, and the architectural fitting of the design to the square or circle of the canvas—would move upward or backward, would anticipate the agility of the cinema, would flow, would disappear into modulated glooms or dissolve into luminosity. In architecture, all is splendor and surprise: polychrome marble, gold coffering, life-size and untranquil statues, ceilings frescoed so as to open the basilican horizontal into a firmament of floating angels, ingenious perspectives, façades designed not to reveal the construction but to be, in themselves, impressive.[6]

The baroque was the Catholic counterstatement to the reformer's attacks on the wealth of the Church and her use of painting and sculpture. Uncommitted

to any single style in architecture or the fine arts, the
Church found in the baroque appeal to the senses a
mode compatible with her tradition.

Protestant and Catholic attitudes towards the arts
differ significantly. The one will have no "graven
images" of the supernatural; probably Hebrew in its
origin, it reappears in Mohammedanism, in icono-
clastic movements, in Calvinism; for it, the senses
are seductive—instruments of the flesh, enemies of
the spirit. The other—more ancient, more indulgent
—incorporates elements of Greek polytheism and
Platonism; it sees a ladder of ascent from beautiful
things to beautiful minds and beautiful souls, and,
finally, to that unchanging Beauty which is, if not
God, then in God. It sees the Incarnation not only as
an event in time but as a sanctification of the body and
the senses.

Catholicism has persistently affirmed that, as the
body, the senses, the affections, and the imagination
are integral parts of man, they must all collaborate
in God's service; that the lower may officiate as
instruments to the higher. Inner humility is not
hindered but assisted by genuflection; kissing the
crucifix, while the imagination engages itself upon
Calvary, stirs the emotions of pity and penitence and
habituates the devout to patience in their own pains.

God transcends all fitting homage, to be sure, as
He transcends all human comprehension. What, for
devotion and for worship, follows? Should men
therefore relinquish all efforts at a theology or a

cultus? Catholicism has long ago given its negative. God stands in no need of human gifts; but, since men would avow their gratitude, express their aspirations and their homage, let them offer of their best, as, to the Infant Jesus, the shepherds presented lambs, and the kings, gold, frankincense, and myrrh. If the heavenly palaces unimaginably surpass all houses built by human hands, let men, at any rate, rear for God a cathedral to overtop their cottages; let all the arts enrich and adorn the sanctuary.

What Catholicism desired for homage to God, the Renaissance desired for its witness to the dignity of man. It coveted splendor in the ceremonial of court: parades, pageants, theatric spectacles, the monumental and magnificent in architecture.[7]

It was the office of the Counter-Reformation to gratify all Renaissance appetites not directly pagan and to extend still further, in opposition to Protestant censure, the traditional Catholic employment of the arts.

In this extension, the Jesuits, exponents of the new Catholicism, had dominance; and the *Spiritual Exercises* of St. Ignatius, the influence of which was, throughout Europe, profound, authorized the "Application of the Senses" to all the themes of religion. The *Exercises*, designed to occupy a month, devote successive weeks to meditation upon sin and the hell which awaits the impenitent, the life of Christ, His sufferings and crucifixion, and the Resurrection and Ascension into the heaven where eternal joy awaits the holy. At the beginning of each meditation, the imagination is invited to see, hear, smell, taste, and feel the outward lineaments of that which it contemplates. For example, the prelude to the fifth day's exercise, *meditatio de Inferno,* is a "compositio": the envisaging of Hell in its length, breadth, and depth. Then, in turn, the senses are invoked: "The first point consists in this, that I see with the eye of the imagination those enormous fires, and the souls as it were in bodies of fire. The second point consists in this, that I hear with the ears of the imagination the lamentations, howlings, cries, the blasphemies against our Lord and against all His Saints. The third point consists in this, that I smell with the sense of smell of the imagination the smoke, brimstone, refuse and rotting things of hell. The fourth point consists in this, that I taste with the sense of taste of the imagination the bitter things, the tears, sorrow, and the worm of conscience in hell. The fifth point consists in feeling with the sense of touch of the imagination how these fires fasten upon and burn souls." [8]

Not to all the themes of contemplation could the complete range of the senses be applied; and naturally, the sight took preëminence, since, for truths purely abstract, it alone could devise symbols. If the theme be the birth of Christ, then the scene must be visualized: the stable, the manger; but if it be the misery of sin, then the imagination may picture a soul imprisoned in the body, banished among animals, in this vale of tears.[9] The Ignatian method thus seeks to localize both the historic and the psychological, to realize, in pictorial or symbolic form, the whole of religion.

From such a method, the transition to emblems, *tableaux vivants,* and paintings designed to stir the pious emotions is but slight. An early edition of the *Exercitia* was illustrated with engravings visualizing not only Heaven and Hell but the states of the soul, the virtues and vices, the warfare between good and evil. To illustrate the Seven Deadly Sins, the engraver depicts a man, nearly naked, sitting in a circular stone dungeon, beneath which yawns the bottomless pit of perdition; the culprit is pierced with seven swords, each entering the part of anatomy which is propense to a particular sin, each ending, beyond the hilt, in the head of the bird, beast, or reptile to which the sin is natural—e.g., the goat for *luxuria,* for *superbia* the peacock. The former of the emblems makes palpable and objective a series of abstract processes; the latter brings to the sinner, incapable of realizing the moral horror of sin, a vivid consciousness of how ugly and bestial it is, visualizes the insecurity which is now his, the pains which await him. The lesson addresses the imagination.[10]

Admirably suited to Jesuit use were those Renaissance and *Seicento* arts, the emblem and the *impresa,* two small genres habitually confounded outside of Italy. As distinguished by specialists in definition, the *impresa* or "heroic symbol" was the more esoteric: it might not contain the human form; might not be obvious enough so that ordinary folk could interpret it; its accompanying motto must be in a language other than that spoken by the owner; and it was designed for the use of an individual. In function, it symbolized the character or purpose of an eminent person or gave visual expression to his motto.[11]

The emblem, on the other hand, addressed humanity at large—particularly children, women, citizens; it sought to convey moral and spiritual truths through the medium of pictures drawn not from the life of Christ or the saints but from the inner life of man, bodied forth in metaphors and short allegories. Far less restricted than the *impresa*, it ordinarily portrayed human figures in some symbolic action against a minutely and realistically delineated background; but the whole aim is nonnaturalistic: the figures personify such "faculties" as the soul, such virtues as love; and there is a free use of such palpable properties as the globe, the cross, the heart.[12]

For their art, the emblematists could claim a long ancestry, reaching back to the Egyptian hieroglyphics and, for Christian precedent, to the burning bush and Gideon's fleece and the parables. "An emblem," affirmed Quarles, chief of the English practitioners, "is but a silent Parable. Let not the tender Eye checke, to see the allusion to our blessed Saviour figured, in these Types. In holy Scripture, He is sometimes called a Sower; sometimes a Fisher; sometimes a Physitian: And why not presented so, as well to the eye, as to the eare? Before the knowledge of letters,

God was knowne by *Hierogliphicks;* And, indeed, what are the Heaven, the Earth, nay every Creature, but *Hierogliphicks* and *Emblems* of His Glory?" [13]

Inaugurated by Alciati, whose collection appeared in 1531 and went through a hundred and forty editions during the sixteenth century, the emblem became, in the seventeenth century, a favorite medium of religious instruction. It had long served the purposes of profane love, with Cupid as its prime figure; in 1615, Vaenius issued *Amoris Divini Emblemata,* in which Cupid has yielded to a winged figure very like that of Christ conceived, according to the devotional wont of the Counter-Reformation, as a child. By a similar metamorphosis, the Cyprian goddess of love gives place to the Blessed Virgin or to Anima, the soul desired by Christ.[14]

Jesuits led the other religious orders in exploiting the happy blend of *dulce et utile.* While, for princes and potentates, at whose flattery they excelled, they devised *impresa,* for popular consumption they produced book after book of sacred emblems—accompanied with epigrams, Latin elegiacs, prose commentaries, and patristic quotations.[15] Representative are the *Pia Desideria of* Hermannus Hugo, the *Typus Mundi* of the Antwerp Jesuits, *Cor Jesu Amanti Sacrum, Partheneia Sacra* by the English Jesuit, Henry Hawkins, and *Cardiomorphoseos* by Francesco Pona. From Antwerp, renowned for its engravers, came the *Schola Cordis* and the *Regia Via Crucis,* both by a Benedictine, van Haeften.

The volumes show a propensity either to group
the innumerable emblems under a common theme
or to include in each design a common symbol, thus
affording scope for metaphorical gymnastic. Chesneau's *Orpheus Eucharisticus* limits its theme to
Christ in the Holy Communion; but, as Orpheus by
his song drew all creatures, animate and inanimate, to
follow him, so the new and divine Orpheus must be
represented as commanding and bodying himself
forth in all things. The illustrative emblems therefore range through a hundred types, arranged under
the general headings of *humana sacra, humana
profana, aves* (Chesneau's favorites), *quadrupes,
pisces, serpentes,* and so on down to flowers, plants,
and fruits. As symbols of the Blessed Virgin, the
Partheneia Sacra offers, and illustrates, the garden,
the rose, the lily, the violet, the sunflower, the dew,
the bee, the heavens, the rainbow, the moon, the star,
the olive, the nightingale, the palm, the house, the
hen, the pearl, the dove, the fountain, the mountain,
the sea, the ship, the phoenix, and the swan. Equal
versatility can be displayed by variations upon a
reiterated symbol. In *Typus Mundi,* the mundane
globe appears in each design; in Quarles' *Hieroglyphicks of the Life of Man,* a candle; in the *Regia
Via,* a cross.

In the *Schola Cordis* and the *Cardiomorphoseos,* a
fleshly, palpable heart undergoes all manner of
strangely wonderful operations and transformations.
The *Schola* depicts the soul offering Jesus half a

heart, while her companion, her worldly self, retains the other; depicts the soul trying in vain to fit the round world into the triangular heart; depicts the heart being plowed, tilled, seeded. Frequently the design translates into bluntly visual terms a scriptural metaphor. "Pour out thine heart like water before the face of the Lord" becomes a young woman, the soul, emptying her heart-shaped bottle into a brook, while the divine Eros stands by attentively. "I sleep, but my heart waketh" takes form in the recumbent figure of a virgin who, though the eyes of her body are closed, holds at arm's length a large heart centrally occupied by a large and wide-open eye. The hundred designs in the *Cardiomorphoseos*, among the most grotesque of emblems, show the heart with one eye or, Argus-like, with many eyes; the heart pierced with arrows; the heart as a fortress surmounted by a crucifix and assailed by warrior demons; the heart streaming blood from its pores and refreshing a subjacent garden of flowers; the Sacred Heart exuding drops of blood which fall upon the human heart; the heart as a fountain: streams of water outline a face with nose and eyebrows, from under which large eyes emit tears. An art of bizarre ingenuity, the sacred emblem does not hesitate to translate into visual form any metaphor offered, in poetry, to the ear.[16]

Ut pictura poesis. The connection of the emblem with poetry was, from the start, close: indeed the term often transferred itself from the picture to the epigram which ordinarily accompanied it. Sometimes the epigram prompted the design; frequently—and this must always have been the case with English emblem books, which, like Quarles', only reproduced the plates from Continental collections—the design inspired the verses.[17] For example, under the emblem, from *Schola Cordis*, of the soul endeavoring to fit the globe into the heart, Christopher Harvey, who used the same designs in his *School of the Heart*, wrote:

> The whole round world is not enough to fill
>   The heart's three corners, but it craveth still;
> Only the Trinity, that made it, can
>   Suffice the vast triangled heart of man.[18]

In any case, the same kind of fancy produced both.[19]

Thus the arts reinforced one another. The influence on poetry was not only to encourage the metaphorical habit but to impart to the metaphors a hardness, a palpability which, merely conceived, they were unlikely to possess. And yet the metaphors ordinarily analogized impalpabilities—states of the soul, concepts, abstractions. The effect was a strange tension between materiality and spirituality which almost defines the spirit of the Counter-Reformation; and from this attempt to prove to St. Thomas' fingers the substance of the substantial, baroque drawing and painting take their inception. Many emblems owe their undeniable grotesqueness to the visualization of metaphors, often scriptural, which were not intended so to be visualized. But having received this embodiment, the sensibility becomes acclimated to them, and

the consequence is the production of analogous metaphors in poetry.

The emblem books lent themselves both to the extended and the contracted conceit, to the elaborate
development of one figure or the phantasmagorical
succession of many. If one meditated upon a single
emblem and sought to express it in poetry, the consequence might be a short allegory; if, on the other
hand, one felt the method of such books as the
Orpheus or the *Partheneia,* one would seek a hundred
metaphors to body forth the same object or conception.

Both the emblem and the "conceit" proceed from
the wit, the faculty which discerns analogies, and
shows itself the more witty as the things analogized
are the more separate one from the other. In all this
there may be more prestidigitation, the virtuoso's desire to amaze:

> È del poeta il fin la meraviglia . . .
> Chi non sa far stupir, vada alla striglia! [20]

But the method, employed by the pens of the philosophical or the pious, may own another rationale. The
wit of the poet, that too must be consecrated to God;
le jongleur may perform his feats of agility to honor
the Queen of Heaven. But wit may be more than an
offering: it may be an instrument of vision. With its
discovery of occult couplings, it perhaps penetrates to
the center of the universe, where, however dissimilar
they appear to the unobservant, all things unite.

"What are all creatures but hieroglyphics and emblems of His glory?" As with Quarles, so with the Catholic emblematists, we may be sure, the conception that the universe is ultimately but a vast system of correspondences, a *Mondo Simbolico*, gave coherence and sanctification to the leaps of the devout wit. The wonder which poetry must produce may be not at the wit of its author but at the wit of God, at the fearful and wonderful nature of His creation, at His miracles which change water into wine and sinners into saints, at the divine power of metamorphosis.

CHAPTER FOUR

THE POETRY

FOR ULTIMATE ancestors, the epigram boasts the *Greek Anthology,* that versatile collection of pagan and Christian poems written over a period of nineteen hundred years, and Martial, who preëmpted sovereignty of the form among the Romans. Relative terseness is almost the only quality shared by these two. While satire and "point" are not entirely absent from the *Anthology,* they are obviously not its essence or mark; with Martial, from whom the Renaissance tradition chiefly stems, the epigram becomes "epigrammatic." [1]

Gruter's ample *Delitiae,* collections of the Italian, French, and Netherlandish poets, include, in their repertoires of Renaissance Latin verse, an abundance of epigrams. There are moralizing distichs and quatrains, classical celebrations of Homer, Pindar, Narcissus, Cupid, innumerable epigrams on illustrious persons—the Popes and Cardinals, Thomas More, Erasmus, Sir Philip Sidney, Queen Elizabeth; but, though many of the poets are priests, sacred epigrams are rare among them.

The Latin epigrams of the English schoolmaster, John Owen, collected in 1624, exerted wide influence throughout the century and found translation into

English, French, German, and Spanish. Though blunt and unpolished in comparison, Owen's sacred distichs anticipate Crashaw in their antitheses, their skirmishings upon such words as *vulnera, mors,* and *crux.* Owen writes of Christ's five wounds:

> Pharmaca sunt potius, quam vulnera, vulnera
>   Christi;
> Curat enim plagis vulnera nostra suis.

He can manipulate the paradox: "The death of death hanging on the cross, and the cross of the cross," and again

> The Cross bare Christ, Christ bare the Cross:
>   and thus
> Christ bare the Cross, the Cross Christ: all for
>   us.

The tears of Mary Magdalen invoke a more elaborate conceit.[2]

In the early decades of the seventeenth century, the Society of Jesus produced many Latinists of distinction; and four at least of the Jesuit epigrammatists—Bettinus, Biderman, Remond, and Bauhusius—have importance for Crashaw's ancestry. A handful of examples will illustrate their rhetorical method. Biderman devoted one book of his epigrams to the nine choirs of virgins: the ninth, representing "Virginitas amisa, et per poenitentiam deplorata," includes the Magdalen, St. Mary of Egypt, St. Afra, the converted courtesan of Augusburg, and Thais.

One epigram expounds a painting of the pair, one
with her *insigne* of tears; the other, with hers, the
flames.

> Magdalis insedit mediam, mediam Afra tabel-
>   lam,
>   Ille suis lacrymis, ignibus ille suis.
> Cur tabula, Pictor, contraria ponis in una?
>   Et juxta flammas uda fluenta locas?
> Scilicet Afra sua ne picta cremetur ab igni,
>   Picta suas illi Magdala jungit aquas.[3]

On that favorite theme of Counter-Reformation
art, the Magdalen, Bettinus wrote epigrams. In one,
she is conceived of as the hunter become the prey
(*praedatrix praeda*):

> Magdala, mortales quibus illaquerat amantes
>   Ausa Deum passis illaquerare comis,
> Dum jacit auratos sacra in vestigia casses,
>   Praedatrix praeda fit ipsa suae.

In another, the penitent sinner fishes in the stream of
her own tears: the title exploits the similarity of
"peccatrix" and "piscatrix." For his epigram on Jesus
walking by the sea of Galilee, Bettinus devised an
elaborate conceit: the waters, honored by the Lord's
proximity, and eager to touch Him, rush to the shore,
lick up with their cerulean lips the golden footprints
He has implanted upon the sand, plant wet kisses
upon His divine feet, and, humbly withdrawing, expire in foam, die satisfied.[4]

Versed in the study of Quintilian, Scaliger, and Pontanus, the Jesuit epigrammatists employ a highly sophisticated rhetoric of schemes and tropes, figures verbal and conceptual: parison, paromoion, polyptoton, homoeoteleuton, alliteration; the apostrophe, the rhetorical question, antithesis, personification, metaphor.[5] There results a virtuosity remote alike from eighteenth-century neoclassicism, which has rejected most of these arts as forms of "false wit," and yet more from nineteenth-century romanticism, which identifies poetry with the lyric and prizes, above all, the appearance of spontaneity. Both subsequent ages, though inconsistent in their use of the key word, would reject so mannered a style as *unnatural*.

In the preface to his *Epigrammata*, Crashaw invokes Catullus and, especially, Martial as his ancestors, regretting only, and much, that these poets were the servants of Cupid and Venus, not of the Infant Jesus and His Mother.[6] In practice, however, Crashaw's style found its real models in the Jesuits.

His *Epigrammata Sacra* contained, in its first, or 1634, edition, one hundred and seventy-eight poems, of which the very large majority are quatrains.

Above most of the epigrams, Crashaw has set a reference to the Biblical text which supplied the theme. All of these come from the New Testament exclusive of the Epistles, and the great majority from the Evangelists. Of the twenty-two which are prefaced by no reference to the Scriptures, all, save a distich on the Gunpowder Plot—for November 5

was, strangely, a kind of Anglican holy day—are
meditations on subjects drawn from the Evangelists
and suggested by the Gospels for the Sundays and
other holy days of the Church Year.

In thus restricting themselves to the Gospels,
Crashaw's epigrams form a unique body of sacred
verse. The Catholic poets, like Biderman and
Bauhusius, though akin to Crashaw in style, and
though sharing his devotion to the Child Jesus and
His Mother, chiefly celebrate the latter-day, or ex-
clusively Catholic, saints, virgins, and martyrs. On
the other hand, most English epigrammatists,
whether writing in Latin or in the vernacular—such
writers as Rosse, Saltmarsh, Hoddeston, and Vilvain
—concern themselves almost entirely with Old Testament themes. The contrast is marked and its significance clear: The Puritan exalts the whole Bible,
as of pervasive and equal inspiration. But he dwells
with a special emphasis upon the law and the history
of God's "separate" and "peculiar" people, in whose
conflicts with Egyptians and Philistines he sees parallels to his own with Papists and Prelatists. For the
Catholic, the Bible is but a part of Revelation, of
which Tradition is the other: church history livingly
continues Bible history; chronology does not deter-
mine sainthood. Between these two stood the High
Anglican, drawing his spiritual nourishment chiefly
from the Psalms and the Gospels.[7]

The character of Crashaw's epigrams is metallic
and hard—in contrast to his later Marinistic poetry,

which errs on the side of lushness. The "conceit" is not totally absent, but metaphors are neither frequent nor characteristic. It is a mannered and rhetorical poetry, but the "colors" are given by such figures as paradox, the antithesis, the pun, the maxim.

These figures merge in one another: The paradox ever antithesizes the apparent and the real. The pun distinguishes two senses of the same word. Balanced structure more commonly than not displays the unlikeness of logical opposites.

Sometimes Crashaw seems to employ these figures as rhetorical tricks: the manner appears to propel itself. But ordinarily intent corroborates method. The Christian Scriptures (whether the Gospels or the Epistles) and Christian theology (from St. Augustine to St. Francis of Sales) abound in paradoxes and antitheses—some of which Crashaw appropriated without change, others of which he refurbished or amplified. "He that saveth his life shall lose it," "He who is greatest among you, let him be your servant" are the words of Christ. According to St. Paul, "the wisdom of this world is foolishness with God." The ambiguity of outer and inner, still adherent to our "see," yields, "Eyes have they but they see not." The Beatitudes abound in what impressed their first auditors as paradoxes if not palpable absurdities, reversing, as they did, all Jewish and pagan philosophy. "Blessed are the poor." "Blessed are the meek." "Blessed are ye when men shall revile and persecute you." Christ turned the cross, the symbol of ignominious death, into "hoc signum," the emblem of victory. St. Paul will not glory, save in the cross. Men come to prize and seek suffering and martyrdom, believing that to submit to the pains inflicted by the persecutors of the Church means to win joy, now and for eternity.

Two ways emerge; and the contrast between the broad way and the strait cannot be made too rigorous. Death in life—this is the way of that "world" which men are bidden not to love; life even in death—that is the Christian way. Crashaw is deeply aware—in his epigrams particularly—of this antinomy between the flesh and the spirit, the world and the kingdom of God.

The central paradox of Christian theology is the doctrine of the Incarnation—the union of the Divine and the human, Time and Eternity. The Infinite takes upon itself the lineaments of the finite; the Absolute makes its entrance upon history. The Everlasting of Days becomes an infant, and God a peasant carpenter: "great humility," says Bishop Andrewes, "that the Word should not be able to speak a word, He that thundereth in Heaven cry in a cradle, He that so great and so high should become so little as a child, and so low as a manger." [8] Thence follows the paradoxical relation of Jesus to Mary, that He is at once her son and her father.

The "point" of Crashaw's epigrams lies customarily in some such paradox or antithesis. Christ's death is our salvation: "mors tibi vita mea." That, for Him, there should be "no room in the inn" prompts one of the incarnational paradoxes: "Illi non locus est, quo sine, nec locus est." The Blessed Virgin, nursing her child, needs not look up to see Heaven; rather "Despicit, at coelum sic tamen illa videt." When Christ miraculously multiplies the loaves and fishes, "Pascitur ipse cibus." Of the Good Shepherd, it is observed that He is "the pastor of the pasture too." Prayer often presents a paradox, for Christians must believe that God answers their petitions even when He does not fulfill them. As Crashaw says in one epigram, Christ alone gives joy even when He denies it; he parallels it in another with "Hoc etiam donare fuit, donare negare." The treatment of Satan's temptation—that Christ turn a stone into bread—is somewhat nearer the "conceit." "My food," said Christ elsewhere, "is to do the will of Him who sent me." As it was God's will that His son should fast, not miraculously feed, so for Him "Est panis, panem non habuisse." On the centurion's familiar words, "Non sum dignus," Crashaw meditates that humility won what ambition would have frustrated—Christ's entrance: "He'll be thy guest because he may not be." [9]

Congenial to Crashaw's mind was the doctrine of "passive resistance"—conquest not by taking up arms but by surrendering them. The epigram, on the chaining of Christ, entitled "De Christi contra mundum pugnâ," is summed up in the last verse: "Injecit lictor vincula, et arma dedit." The sufferings of

Christ are the weapons by which He overcomes the world.

For St. Andrew's day, Crashaw exploits the paradox of the fisherman who, though it has ever been his vocation to catch, must now find salvation in being caught by the Divine Fisher: "Artem inverte, et jam tu quoque disce capi."[10]

The conversion of St. Paul, twice Crashaw's text, both times suggests obfuscation by excess of light.

That Paul was blind, I will not say:
Sure Paul was *captus lumine*.

The paradox of an enlightening darkness is again invoked in an epigram on the sick who implore the shadow of Peter (Acts 5:15).

Umbra dabit tua posse meum me cernere
   solem;
Et mea lux umbrae sic erit umbra tuae.[11]

Sometimes the contrasts are verbal, as of the offerings made by the rich and the mite given by the widow: "Isti abjecerunt . . . illa dedit." Sometimes alliterative, as of the miracle of loaves: "Illa [the sacred banquet] *famem* populi pascit, et illa *fidem*." Sometimes harshly elementary, as in the contrast of Jewish and Christian Sabbaths. The wit persists.[12]

Most frequently the contrast is of *inner* and *outer*. The Pharisee boldly enters the temple; the publican stands outside the door, yet is nearer his goal than the other, for he strikes his breast, and it is man's breast which is really the "temple of God." Martha prepares food for Christ, but Mary receives it from her guest: Satan tempts Christ to hurl himself from the temple; ah! but soon Christ will hurl Satan from the human heart. The stones of his persecutors did not wound St. Stephen, but their hard hearts, their stony breasts— those did. On the healing of the man afflicted with dropsy, Crashaw writes, "Pellitur indè sitis; sed et hinc sitis altera surgit." His hydroptic body cured, the thankful man thirsts for the "water of life." [13]

Crashaw sometimes puns. The trembling of the earth at the Crucifixion prompts, "Quod tellus dubitat, vos dubitare vetat," in which the poet first uses the verb in its archaic sense of "vibrate," and then in its habitual sense of "doubt." The *double entendre* of "shade" is addressed to the sick awaiting the healing shadow of St. Peter: "Atque umbras fieri (creditis?) umbra vetat." Zachary, father of John the Baptist, seeks a "sign" and is stricken dumb, so that he can speak only in sign language. Christ, riding into Jerusalem, had to endure the humiliation of being borne by an ass. "Hoc, quòd sic *fertur*, hoc quoque *ferre* fuit." The Infant Martyrs, dying in a flood commingled of their own blood and their mothers' milk, took, on their heavenward journey, the "lactea via." In the epigram, "Ego sum ostium," an effective paronomasia juxtaposes *clavus* (nail) and *clavis* (key)—

Jamque pates. cordisque seram gravis hasta
  reclusit,
Et clavi claves undique te reserant.[14]

Another epigram, "Dominus apud suos vilis," plays
on *consanguine*. The thief on the cross was of the
same blood with Christ in a truer sense than were his
kinsfolk.

En consanguinei! patriis en exul in oris
Christus! *et haud alibi tam peregrinus erat.*
Qui socio demum pendebat sanguine latro,
O consanguineus quàm fuit ille magis! [15]

In a small number of the epigrams, Crashaw de-
parts more boldly from the text of the Gospels and,
following the example of the Jesuit poets, ventures
far-flying conceits. Christ called himself the Vine.
Yes, but a vine needs a trellis: the tree of Calvary
supplies it. "Da fulcrum; fulcrum da mihi: quale?
crucem." Christ followed his parable of the Sower
with an exegesis, according to which the seed is the
Word, the thorns among which some of it fell, the
"cares and riches and pleasures of this world."
Crashaw, choosing to take the seed figuratively and
the thorns literally, derives the "Verbum inter
spinas"—the Logos crowned with thorns. An ingeniously perverse epigram on the withered fig tree
disconnects itself entirely from Christ's curse upon
that which bears no fruit. Rejecting this patently
ethical significance, Crashaw fancies the tree blessed

by the curse, for, though cursed, it was cursed by
Christ, addressed—that is—by Christ; blessed, too,
in being an occasion for the Lord to display His miraculous power. Very similar is Crashaw's treatment
of the tempest on the sea which Christ stilled. Barksdale translates:

> That the sea with such violence falls on
> 'Tis not his malice, but ambition.
> At Thy command, O Christ, to take his rest.[16]

An epigram on the healing of the man with dropsy
has already been cited. Crashaw treated the theme
again with more elaborate ingenuity. Beginning with
the initial conceit of the man who was "his own
ocean," and fusing the miraculous cure with the
miracle performed at Cana, Crashaw interprets the
joy of the man as drunkenness caused by the trans-
formation of *his* waters into wine.

In another epigram, the water of the Magdalen's
tears cleanses Christ's feet; the flame of her hair dries
it. The water is cleansed by the dirt it removed; the
fire glows more brightly for its contact with the
water.[17]

Finally, a few of the epigrams are built on sanguinary metaphors so characteristic of Crashaw's later
poems and so repugnant to normal taste. "On the
Wounds of Christ," Crashaw meditates, are these
mouths or eyes? To answer, both: "O nimium roseis
florentia labris." In the epigram on the Circumcision, the faithful are bidden to drink the blood.

"Beatus venter et ubera" suggests to him the relationship: Christ drank milk from Mary's breasts; soon she will drink blood from her son's. And in the celebrated epigram on the Holy Innocents, milk becomes lilies; blood, roses.[18]

Crashaw's Latin epigrams, the work of one who had mastered the rhetorical discipline, are far more than the perfunctory discharge of an obligation imposed by the terms of a college scholarship and more than the scales and arpeggios of an apprentice poet. During the years when English schools and colleges required the composition of Latin quatrains on the Gospel for the Day, innumerable youths must, with pious conscientiousness, have filled their manuscript-books; but, of all this diligence, Crashaw's epigrams alone possessed the brilliance and maturity to invite publication.[19] Distinguished of style they are: the best Latin epigrams written by an Englishman. Nor will a diligent search through the neglected volumes of Renaissance Neo-Latinity discover any master of whom Crashaw is not peer. To English poetry, they hardly belong—not only or chiefly because their language is that of all educated Europe, but because, though they restrict themselves in theme to the New Testament and never transcend the theology of High Anglicanism, their method was borrowed from the Jesuits, and their spirit is that of the Counter-Reformation.

Within the concentration of the epigram, Crashaw could manipulate, and manipulate brilliantly, those figures which were for him not tropes merely but, rather, characteristic forms of vision—the metaphor, the antithesis, the paradox. There were, however, other elements in his nature which needed forms of expression more expansive, forms admitting of fluidity, cumulative ardor. To follow the course of his poetry is to move, hesitatingly but with a felt sense of direction, from the epigram to the ode.

2. THE SECULAR POEMS AND TRANSLATIONS

CRASHAW's secular poems, less ardent than the devotional odes of his final period, witness to the sensuousness and the fastidious elegance of his temperament; "Music's Duel" apart, none of them touches the ecstasy to which religion was to fire him, or, rather, in none of them does he sustain ecstasy through the length of a poem. *The Delights of the Muses,* written during his undergraduate years, experiment in a variety of modes, rhythmic and imagistic, such as an acquaintance with the fecund productions of the "last age" could afford. The essential in Crashaw, his religious devotion subtracted, was a fascinated concern for style, a literary Alexandrianism like that of Bion and Moschus or Pater or Flaubert, an intense pleasure in the manipulation of words and figures, a delicacy of the senses which probably made the imitative arts preferable to nature's more violent administrations, which made books, pictures, and music the normal stimuli to composition.

In the *Delights,* the subject of the poem matters little. Crashaw could write at length and exquisitely on the Gunpowder Plot. Almost all the verses are either translations or "occasional" elegies on the eminent or not so eminent who have just been translated from the University into some gracious Cambridge of the skies.

By contrast with the poetry of the Elizabethans, the themes are restricted, for Crashaw eschews three subjects normal and, in Elizabethan poetry, ubiquitous. He never sang the sexual passions; he wrote none of those at once exact and honorific descriptions of the female body such as one finds in Spenser, in Sidney, in the "Compliment" and "Rapture" of his contemporary, Carew. His "Wishes" invoke no breasts, and even the smiles of his hypothetical mistress are such "that chastity shall take no harm." Again, though he wrote elegies, he never gives us the "metaphysical shudder" of Donne and Marvell, never that sudden abrupt shift from life to death of "at my back I always hear," never the complex of love and death in "whoever comes to shroud me." The thought of death was, to full-blooded Elizabethans, painful; the prospect of physical dissolution dismayed and fascinated dramatists and lyric poets alike. With Crashaw it was not so. Caring little for life, he did not fear the grave; his friends could never wish him "joy of the worm"; he rarely, with Horace and Herrick, meditates upon the brevity of life, pained that the lovely should be so fragile.

Though he uses the *word* constantly, "death" is, for him, a ritual and mystical term; and his oxymora, *living death* and *dying life,* are but testimonies to unconcern for the fate of the body.

Crashaw has, finally, almost none of that intense, fresh, observant pleasure in Nature which enables Spenser and Shakespeare and Milton to make poetry out of a botanist's catalogue—

> The tufted crow-toe and pale jessamine
> The white pink and the pansy freak'd with jet,
> The glowing violet. . . .

Carew, man of the court and habitually given to imagery from jewels and spices rather than from garden and woodland, now and then walks out. His "Spring" opens with four lines in which the metaphors are as palpably artificed as, two of them, grotesquely indoor:

> Now that the Winter's gone, the earth has lost
> Her snow-white *robes,* and now no more the frost
> *Candies* the grass, or casts an icy *cream*
> Upon the *silver* lake or *crystal* stream.

With the next line, however, the mode alters to that of a Collins freed of his tumid diction or of a terser Wordsworth.

> But the warm sun thaws the benumbed earth
> And makes it tender; gives a sacred birth

> To the dead swallow; wakes in hollow tree
> The drowsy cuckoo and the humble-bee.[20]

To these lines, Crashaw's "Descriptio Veris" offers nothing comparable. After a prelude of generalities, Zephyr, Flora, and Venus are introduced; and the remainder of the graceful poem conjectures, fancifully, the springtime employment of Venus' host of little cupids. Almost unique, in Crashaw's verse, is the strophe, written in 1631,

> I've seen indeed the hopefull bud,
> Of a ruddy Rose that stood
> Blushing, to behold the Ray
> Of the new-saluted Day:
> (His tender toppe not fully spread)
> The sweet dash of a shower now shead,
> Invited him no more to hide
> Within himself, the purple pride
> Of his forward flower . . .[21]

and its isolation makes one suspect that somewhere in Latin poetry a simile like Catullus' "ut flos in saeptis secretus nascitur hortis" had suggested this fresh delicacy. Two poems, "To Morning" and "On a Foul Morning," also without counterparts, seem to have had their inception in real feeling for the dawn and light; but in both the impulse which would have prompted an Elizabethan to portraiture is elaborately overlaid with literary decoration.

These absences narrow the appeal of Crashaw's

Delights. By way of substitution, however, many "serious" readers would accept what they desire from poetry as well as prose—moral fervor or moral indignation. But Crashaw was neither didactic nor satiric in his genius. His few attempts—a translation from Martial, in which he tries to work himself up to a salt harshness alien to his nature, his school-boy exercises like "Thesaurus malorum Femina"—seem early to have convinced him that these kinds lay outside his scope. Nowhere does his work provide counterpart to such admirable versified commonplace as Wotton's "Character of a Happy Life" or Pomfret's "The Choice" or Wordsworth's "Happy Warrior"; his poetry preserves its "purity" and exists for the innocent delectation of the senses.

In search of antecedents for this art-poetry, one can limit himself chiefly to considerations of versification and imagery. Crashaw acknowledged no English master, contributed no memorial to *Jonsonius Virbius,* no elegy on the death of Dr. Donne. Of English poets, he mentions only Ford and Sidney; his "Sidneian showers of sweet discourse," in "Wishes," is so unparalleled as to make one attach a perhaps undue importance to it; and whether he is recollecting the Euphuistic prose of the *Arcadia* or the poems, it is impossible to tell.

The Spenserian stanza he nowhere imitates, even in the sundry truncated forms devised by the Fletchers. Perhaps, with his strongly marked preference for couplets, he shared the judgment of his friend, Beaumont, that Spenser himself was shackled by the complication of his rhyme scheme.[22] The descriptive style of the *Faerie Queene* must, for Crashaw's taste, have seemed diffuse and thin, the imagery not crowded enough, and decorative rather than symbolic, the simile too dilated and too little researched. Even Spenser's music would be somewhat too low-pitched, too sparse of overtones.

With a few exceptions, Crashaw's secular poems restrict themselves, in versification, to the couplet, tetrameter or pentameter. That he wrote no sonnets is not surprising, since, for his contemporaries as well, the form was outmoded; but, though Carew, Suckling, and Lovelace all used the couplet easily and often, they did their best work, as did Donne and George Herbert, in a variety of ingenious stanzas. The great proponent of the heroic couplet was Ben Jonson; and the tetrameter couplet, not uncommon with Greene and Breton and in the songs of Shakespeare, served Jonson as a favorite lighter measure in both *The Forest* and *Underwoods*, notably in the "Celebration of Charis":

> Such my Mothers blushes be
> As the Bath your verse discloses
> In her cheekes, of Milke, and Roses;
> Such as oft I wanton in:
> And, above her even chin,
> Have you plac'd the banke of kisses,
> Where, you say, men gather blisses,

> Rip'ned with a breath more sweet
> Than when flowers, and West-winds meet.[23]

The tercet, of which Crashaw's "Wishes" is a variant, occurs frequently in Jonson's lyrics; the poem itself may have been suggested by its counterpart, "Her Man Described by her own Dictamen," in which Charis describes her supposed lover.

Crashaw's stylistic evolution can be traced within the compass of the *Delights*, moving gradually, though with many anticipations and reversions, from the elegies on Brook and Herrys[24] to the luxuriance of "Music's Duel." Nearest to Jonson are the elegies, written during the poet's first year at Pembroke, and, by comparison with Crashaw's work of a few years later, sparingly imaged. The first of the Herrys poems offers but one basic figure, that of a tree in first blossom, which, before the expected fruit has time to appear, is overturned by the wind, though its roots still live; the third offers, in leisurely development, the Renaissance analogy between life and a book. All four contain a surprising amount of "prose statement"; and some of the finest effects are secured by the use of a single felicitous epithet, the dexterous variation of the pauses or management of the cadence:

> Softly may he be possest
> Of his *monumentall* rest.
> Safe, thou darke home of the dead,
> Safe O hide his loved head.[25]

The elegy "On the Death of a Gentleman," probably written in 1634, achieves something of the same effect. In the closing lines of "To the Morning," the imagery is subdued, the antithesis unostentatious, the style classical.

> Bestow thy Poppy upon wakefull woe,
> Sicknesse, and sorrow, whose pale lidds ne're
>   know
> Thy downy finger, dwell upon their Eyes,
> Shut in their Teares; Shut out their miseryes.[26]

"Wishes to his Supposed Mistress" is Crashaw's chief piece in the manner of the Jonsonians; it can be read with pleasure by those who find his later and more personal idiom repellent. Prose statement, gracefully turned, finds decoration in imagery and similes neither extravagant nor researched.

> Feares, fond and flight,
> As the coy Brides, when Night
> First does the longing lover right.

> Teares, quickly fled,
> And vaine, as those are shed
> For a dying Maydenhead.

A delicate and accomplished performance, justly favorite, the poem might have been composed by any one of the young Elizabethan or Jacobean poets and, save in a few stanzas, would elicit no ready identification.

These simpler images, this restrained music, seem, though he never lost his power to command them, not to have satisfied Crashaw: they represent distinctly an "earlier manner."

Like Donne, he owned two Muses, a profane and a sacred; as with Donne, Urania was the final victor; and, as with Donne, the two show a family likeness.[27] There the comparison almost stops. Donne's youthful cynicism and perhaps profligacy, the misfortunes which followed his unsanctioned marriage, his worldly ambitions, only after combat with himself transmuted into ascetic piety, his strain of scepticism, his hydroptic passion for such learning, new and old, as would offer him strange perspectives, his bent for introspection and for dialectic casuistry, whether in love or in religion, his fear of death and his ominous shroud, his restless aspirations which never found complete satisfaction: all these dramatic characters found no counterpart in the experiences or the nature of Crashaw. By contrast, Crashaw had an epicure's instinctive feeling for his métier. His intellect was neither speculative nor subtle; almost purely a creature of sensibility, he possessed and developed and refined his emotions, undisturbed by the vast exclusions they necessitated.

In style, Donne's tokens are his rugged versification; his relish for abrupt beginnings; the close, dialectic texture of the whole poem; and his "conceits"—that is, his metaphors, now terse, now developed, but drawn always from terrains little mined by the other Elizabethans—physics, geometry, law, divinity—metaphors more abstract or recondite than that which they analogized. By contrast, Crashaw's versification is shiningly smooth; his structure, save when furnished by others, lacks tightness; his metaphors are sensuous and external.

That both poets had the courage of their arts and reached for figures which the nineteenth century would have rejected: so much warrant there was for assigning Crashaw to the following of Donne. Brief passages, in the elegy on Mr. Staninough and elsewhere, seem to show a closer relation. The defense of "Hope," written in paragraph by paragraph reply to Cowley's hypothetical scepticism, takes its ten-line stanza and most of its images and figures from its Cowleyan model.[28] A kind of poetic counterpart to the ingenious disputations which formed a favorite academic exercise at the universities, its matching of thesis with counterthesis draws Crashaw into a few lines of Scholastic language, as when he writes of Hope that it is

> The entity of things that are not yet.
> Subtlest, but surest being! Thou by whom
> Our nothing has a definition.

Donnean is his simile for the passage of dawn into day. The differences between Cowley, vicar for Donne, and Crashaw are quite as marked: the latter's characteristic parisons, oxymora, and alliterations have no warrant from the former. Closest to Donne in structure is "Love's Horoscope," the title of which suggests Donne's series of "Love's Exchange," "Love's Alchemy," "Love's Diet," "Love's Usury." The poem is built, in a fashion uncommon with Crashaw, upon a single "conceit": The stars ordinarily control men's destinies; but the lover's fate is in the power of his mistress' eyes, the stars of a new astrology; and whatever the heavens may dictate, her rays alone can bid him live or die. And the poem has a syntactical tightness, a marshaling of "if" and "but" and "while" and "for," the connective implements of ratiocination, which is reminiscent of Donne. The refrain, the alliteration and conventional rhetoric of the last two stanzas, the glossier diction forming a medium through which the "conceit" is passed, diminish the resemblance. Crashaw's total indebtedness to Donne is slight.[29]

The elegy on Staninough, written in 1634 and one of the few undergraduate pieces to be retained in the final selection, *Carmen Deo Nostro*, tries a variety of styles.

> Dear reliques of a dislodg'd soule, whose lacke
> Makes many a mourning Paper put on blacke;
> O stay a while e're thou draw in thy Head,
> And wind thy selfe up close in thy cold Bed:
> Stay but a while, untill I call
> A summons, worthy of thy Funerall.
>   Come then youth, Beauty, and Blood, all ye
>   soft powers,

Whose silken flatteryes swell a few fond houres
Into a false Eternity, come man,
(Hyperbolized nothing!) know thy span.
Take thine own measure here, downe, downe,
    and bow
Before thy selfe in thy Idæa, thou
Huge emptinesse contract thy bulke, and shrinke
All thy wild Circle to a point! . . .

. . . .

These curtain'd windowes, this selfe-prison'd
    eye,
Out-stares the Liddes of large-look't Tyranny.
This posture is the brave one: this that lyes
Thus low stands up (me thinkes) thus, and
    defyes
The world—All daring Dust and Ashes; onely
    you
Of all interpreters read nature true.[30]

The first six lines might have been written by Henry
King, whose elegies blend Jonson's versification with
an infusion of Donne's imagery and a tincture of his
shudder. Of Donne there is a hint in the geometric
figure of the circle contracting to a point and in the
use of Idea in its Platonic sense. But later the poem
takes a melodramatic tone, most marked in the reit-
eration of "down"; the movement of the lines is
staccato; the caesuras occur frequently and at unex-
pected places. The reader hears, in short, a rhymed
version of some speech from the fifth act of some

Jacobean dramatist; and one recalls that Crashaw knew the tragedies of Ford.[31]

Concurrently with these accomplished studies in rhythm and imagery, Crashaw continued the practice, begun at Charterhouse, of turning Latin and Greek verses into English. Indeed, most of his secular poetry, like most of Drummond's,[32] bears some relation to an original outside itself.

"Translation" is too inflexible a term to serve; not even Roger Ascham's distinctions of translation, paraphrase, metaphrase, and imitation provide for the final category in such a series—transfusion.[33] Until the nineteenth century, men of letters felt no squeamish fears of plagiarism, no scrupulous concern for an originality running the gamut from fable to sentiments and from sentiments to metaphors. Chaucer and Shakespeare borrowed their plots; Spenser and Milton appropriated incidents, scenes, images, phrases, obeyed Vida's counsel to "steal boldly," confident that the force of their personality and the skill of their art were sufficient to assimilate their acquisitions; Pope and Johnson creatively imitated satires of Horace and Juvenal and rewrote, in the modern manner, selected pieces from Chaucer and Donne. The attitude and the practice went back of the vernacular literatures to the Roman poets, who, even Vergil, Catullus, and Horace, imitated the Greeks. In back of this attitude were principles often expounded by the rhetoricians: Each vernacular literature, they argued, should be enriched by the incorporation into

it of ancient and foreign wealth, a motive at once
patriotic and humane; indebtedness justified itself
when it put the loan out to productive interest, im-
proved or significantly altered; since many of the
original beauties, dependent upon idiom or the music
of the language, cannot be reproduced, the translator
of poetry should provide new beauties of his own;
translation, when practiced by a poet rather than by
a scholarly commentator, should aim not at literal
fidelity but at a poem capable of giving pleasure in
its own right, such a poem as the author, "if he were
living, and an Englishman . . . would probably
have written." [34]

Crashaw's "translations" vary much in their degree
of closeness to their originals. Almost certainly, the
most literal of them—those from Vergil's *Georgics*
and Heliodorus, for example—are the earliest, re-
mainders from much apprentice work at Charterhouse; and the comparative awkwardness of the style
in the former, the sense it gives of moving conscientiously from phrase to phrase and line to line,
suggests a careful reliance on the text before the
translator. Three subsequent versions from the classics—the "Cupids Cryer" of Moschus, the fifth ode
of Catullus, and the thirteenth from the Second
Book of Horace's odes—show Crashaw more at ease,
more confident of his powers. Though for the most
part following his text, he allows his fancy to add an
occasional embellishment. Horace writes: "penetra-
lia/sparsisse nocturno cruore/hospitis"; and Crashaw,

recasting the whole, adds a line unwarranted by
Horace:

> that mans barbarous knife
> Conspir'd with darkness 'gainst the strangers
> throat
> (Whereof the blushing walls tooke bloody
> note).

In that celebrated ode which Ben Jonson twice paraphrased, Catullus wrote: "nobis cum semel occidit
brevis lux, / nox est perpetua dormienda." The elegant tenderness of these lines Crashaw appreciated;
but, unemulous of their simplicity, he retouched
them, adding alliterative appositive for *nobis* and
double personification.

> But if we darke sons of sorrow
> Set; o then, how long a Night
> Shuts the Eyes of our short light.

The paraphrase from Grotius' *Christus Patiens*,
eighty-six lines upon a text of sixty-three, admits still
further latitude of interlinear decoration.[35]

In spite of their liberties, the pieces thus far named
were conceived by Crashaw as translations. The same
is true of three lyrics labeled "out of the Italian."
One, the charming "Song," reproduces the rhyme
scheme, the persistently feminine endings, and the
metrical pattern of the original, by Ansaldo Ceba:

Dispiegate
Guance amate
Quella porpora acerbetta;
Che perdenti
Che dolenti
Fian le rose in su l'herbetta

To thy Lover
Deere, discover
That sweet blush of thine that shameth
(When those Roses
It discloses)
All the flowers that Nature nameth.[36]

With "Music's Duel" the case is different. It bears no titular mark of derivation; yet it, too, had a text: in the *Prolusions* (1617) of the Jesuit professor of rhetoric, Famianus Strada, who offered his poem as an "imitation" of Claudian's style.[37] In studying the relationship between the two, one is first struck with the disparity in length: Strada's "Fidicinis et Philomelae Bellum Musicum" runs to fifty-eight lines; Crashaw's, to a hundred and sixty-eight, almost thrice the length. Through the first fourteen lines, Crashaw follows Strada with fair fidelity as though it had been his original intention to produce a translation; but Crashaw's maturing powers found any persistent effort at literal fidelity unexciting, and the final relation between the two poems is one of structure.

The musical virtuosity of the nightingale was a favorite theme of sixteenth- and seventeenth-century writers. Sandys disserts on it in the notes to his translation of Ovid. Du Bartas (whose *Semaine*, in Sylvester's paraphrase, Crashaw assuredly knew) celebrated at length the bird

> Breathing so sweetly from a brest so small,
> So many Tunes, whose Harmony excels
> Our Voyce, our Violls, and all Musick els.[38]

According to the Jesuit, Henry Hawkins, the nightingale's "usual songs are certain Catches and Roundelayes he hath. . . . You would take him verily to be a Monsieur of Paris streight, if you heard but his preludiums; for then indeed is he set upon a merrie pin. Sometimes againe wil he be in a melancholy dump, and strike you such Notes as *Dowland* himself never strock, in al his Plaints and Lachrymies." [39] These early notes upon the nightingale contrast strikingly, in their dispassionate and professional assessment of its artistic endowment, with Keats' self-absorption, so complete that the bird becomes only a stimulus to autobiography.

Strada's addition to the current stock was a fable, the brief tale of a love-sick young man who, playing upon his lute, attracts the rivalry of the woodland's chief singer. Twice he displays his skill; twice she responds with equal. This third performance, to which, angered, he applies vigor and violence, is pathetically triumphant; for the nightingale, over-taxing herself, dies, falling upon the lute.[40] A fable calculated to charm lovers of music, it attracted attention surprising when one considers that it made its first appearance in a Jesuit's lectures on rhetoric. Marino retold it in seventeen octaves of his *Adone*, adding, as refinement to the conclusion, that the musician buried the bird in the lute and wrote, with one her feathers, the tale of the duel; the tale reappears, briefly, in the first act of Ford's *Lover's Melancholy*, where Crashaw may first have encountered it; ten or twelve other English versions exist out of what must have been a much larger number of imitations.[41]

In some of these versions, including Ford's, the sadly sweet tale is the thing; not so with Marino and Crashaw, supreme descriptive and decorative artists, for both of whom Strada supplied simple architecture to be filled in and covered over with elaborate detail. For both, "Musica e Poesia son due sorelle" [42] was the complementary maxim to "Ut pictura poesis." Both loved music; both had some knowledge of music and its terminology; both—what does not necessarily follow—sought, by onomatopeia and subtler forms of tone color, to create a poetry approximating music.

Crashaw's technical terms, his *praeludium, divisions, diapason,* are fewer than those to be found in Marino or Milton and can be matched by many of his contemporaries in an age when musicianship, to the extent of reading at sight one's part in a madrigal and playing the lute, was an expected accomplishment of gentlemen.[43] He makes some onomatopoeic representations of sound: the strings "grutch and murmur in a buzzing dinne": the bass *grumbles;* the treble *chirps;* there is the harshness of "warr's hoarce Bird." But poetry's limit in the more or less exact reproduction of sound is soon reached, even when written by Crashaw or Lanier. "Musical" poetry cannot offer the range of pitch, volume, and timbre accessible to the organ and the symphony; and when literary critics borrow the language of music, speak of melody, harmony, counterpoint, and the like, they use the terms metaphorically for poetry's equivalents. Commonly, poetry is said to be "musical" when it avoids hiatus, harsh combinations of consonants, and explosive "stops," and eschews abrupt shifts of rhythm; when it makes large use of "liquids" and sonorous vowels and feminine rhyme; when, by the employment of consonantal and vowel sequences, word glides into word as though, independent of the sense, sounds had a magnetism of their own. In this sense, and by the employment of these techniques, Marino and Crashaw are almost invariably musical; their pieces could be heard with pleasure as songs without words.

But, when all these resources have been employed, verse still fails to offer the equivalent of any save the more minor and dulcet strains. Poetry is a mixed art: reduced to aping music, she is unequal to her model; reduced to painting in words, she cannot equal the colors and the chiaroscuro of the canvas. Of this, Crashaw was conscious; and "Music's Duel," in its endeavor to produce an emotional effect equal to that which, undoubtedly he gained from music, augments auditory with visual imagery and with the vaguer imagery of the other senses. Crashaw's method is best studied in lines 57 to 156, which, corresponding to but fifteen of Strada's, are almost completely his own.

> Then starts shee suddenly into a Throng
> Of short thicke sobs, whose thundring volleyes float,
> And roule themselves over her lubricke throat
> In panting murmurs, still'd out of her Breast
> That ever-bubling spring; the sugred Nest
> Of her delicious soule, that there does lye
> Bathing in streames of liquid Melodie;
> Musicks best seed-plot, whence in ripend Aires
> A Golden-headed Harvest fairely reares
> His Honey-dropping tops, plow'd by her breath
> Which there reciprocally laboureth
> In that sweet soyle. It seemes a holy quire
> Founded to th' Name of great *Apollo's* lyre.
> Whose sylver-roofe rings with the sprightly notes
> Of sweet-lipp'd Angell-Imps, that swill their throats
> In creame of Morning *Helicon*. . . .

The sentence structure is loose, the short predication trailing off into a voluminous series of appositives to which, in turn, are attached unrestrictive clauses; the limit of appositives seems dependent only upon the fecundity of the fancy. In the course of the metaphorical exercise, the bird's breast becomes a distilling retort, a spring of water, a nest (which becomes a bath), a plot of ground, plowed, seeded, and harvested, and the choir of a silver-vaulted cathedral, in which, as choristers, officiate plump cherubs whose voices have been lubricated with the "top" of the dew which covers the mountain whence issue the springs dear to Apollo and the Muses. The reader is invited to hear the music, and also to see it, to sniff its sweet odor, to swill its cream and its sugar, to float upon its streams of melody.

Between this sort of sensuous presentation and that of Keats' "Eve of St. Agnes" there is a sharp distinction. Crashaw's lacks the narrative element and the "human interest" which, in Keats' poem, mitigate or variegate the description. But, more basically, Keats is describing things—things to look at and to taste and to touch, and describing each in language proper to each sense; Crashaw is not really describing any *thing* but providing metaphorical equivalents for the feelings aroused in him when he listens to music, and, with what seems almost like aesthetic system, he translates from sense to sense till all are blended and confounded in a common sensibility.

"Music's Duel" is the secular triumph of the Crashavian style, and it remains, of its kind, the most impressive achievement in English poetry.

3. THE SACRED MUSE OF MARINISM

Altera Cypris habet nos; habet alter Amor.
Scilicet hic Amor est; hic est quoque Mater Amoris
Sed Mater virgo; sed neque caecus Amor.[44]

The preface to *Epigrammata Sacra* is Crashaw's
valediction to the Cyprian Venus; and, save for addresses to the pious and divinely appointed royal family of Charles, he wrote, thereafter, no secular poetry.
Aware of their contemporaries, the "madrigall
fellowes, whose onely businesse in verse, is to rime a
poore six-penny soule, a Subburb sinner into hell," [45]
the sacred poets of Tudor and Stuart England rarely
offered their poems to the public without some prefatory antithesis between the profane love and sacred,
between the pagan muses and the Christian muse,
Urania. Often they contrast the rival founts and the
rival mounts,[46] as Lloyd wrote of Crashaw that he had
"no other *Helicon*, than the *Jordan* of his eyes; nor
Parnassus, than the *Sion* where dwelled his thoughts,
that made the Muses Graces. . . ." [47] There was
requisite a double defense—against the worldling,
who desired poetry to be his amusement, the titillation
of his wantonness, for whom the recollection of the
supernatural backdrop was a rebuke; against, also,
the Puritan, for whom the sacred realities were matters for reason and faith, too solemn for adornment,
and not to be explored or exploited by the imagination.

By way of reply to such as "thinke it halfe sacrilege for prophane poetrie to deale with divine and heavenly matters," Giles Fletcher appealed to his honorable predecessors: Moses, David, and Solomon, St. Gregory Nazianzen, who metrically celebrated the Genealogy, the Miracles, the Parables, and the Passion of Christ, "sedulous Prudentius" and "prudent Sedulius," St. Bernard, Sannazaro, du Bartas, Edmund Spenser.[48]

In espousing the cause of sacred poetry, there was, for Crashaw, the immediate sanction of Donne and Herbert. That the title of his 1646 volume was a confession of indebtedness to Herbert, of avowed imitation, is not, however, the case. Crashaw knew and cherished *The Temple;* but, though his follower in time, he was Herbert's equal in poetic authority; he seems to have valued Herbert as him who "hath retriv'd Poetry of late, and return'd it up to its Primitive use; let it bound back to heaven gates, whence it came." These words, from the preface to Crashaw's volume—possibly by Joseph Beaumont—are followed by the declaration that the poems are steps to the Temple of God, "Stepps for happy soules to climbe heaven by." Neither in versification nor in imagery does Crashaw derive from Herbert; only in a single poem, "Charitas Nimia," does Crashaw invoke recollection of Herbert's temper and spirit. Herbert's poems are autobiographical, lyrics born from the wrestlings of his soul with God; Crashaw's are devotional and objective.[49]

The Divine Poems have more passion, more intensity, than Herbert's; but their masculinity, their dialectic, their abrupt rhythms, their range of figures, separate them from Crashaw. Donne seems most nearly ancestral in "The Cross," one of his own least characteristic poems.

>   the losse
> Of this Crosse, were to mee another Crosse;
> Better were worse, for, no affliction,
> No Crosse is so extreme, as to have none.
> Who can blot out the Crosse, which th'
>   instrument
> Of God, dew'd on mee in the Sacrament?
> Who can deny mee power, and liberty
> To stretch mine armes, and mine owne Crosse
>   to be?
> Swimme, and at every stroake, thou art thy
>   Crosse;
> The Mast and the yard make one, where seas
>   do tosse;
> Looke downe, thou spiest out Crosses in small
>   things;
> Looke up, thou seest birds rais'd on crossed
>   wings. . . .[50]

If one reads on, he will come—even in this poem so concentrated on the ingenious application of a single figure, now metaphor and now pun—upon figures alien to Crashaw, figures drawn from medicine, physiology, and alchemy. But even in these lines, the homely ruggedness of the style minimizes the ingenuity of the fancy; the flavor is individual or personal; we look down and up, not into Hell and Heaven, but into a world patent to the body's eye. Even on this, the most Christian and traditional of themes, Donne holds fast to his own self-consciousness; he sinks neither himself nor his style into communion with his fellow worshipers. Even the cross is his cross, and the cross of denying himself rather than the cross on Calvary from which streamed blood sufficient to save all the sinners that ever were or shall be.

Two older kinsmen in spirit and style, English poetry could supply: Robert Southwell and Giles Fletcher—one a Jesuit, the other an Anglican priest. Southwell, Elizabethan martyr to his faith, wrote poetry in two modes—the former, simple, relatively unadorned, moral and moralizing rather than religious, of which "Content and Rich" and "Loss in Delay" may suffice as samples; the latter, definitely rhetorical and definitely Catholic. Of the second kind, the themes are Christ—His Circumcision, His Bloody Sweat, the Blessed Sacraments; the style is alliterative, paradoxical, metaphorical.

Saint Peter's Complaint (1595), Southwell's masterpiece, celebrates the apostle's penitence for his denial of Christ. Twenty stanzas, metaphorically versatile, are devoted to the Saviour's eyes: They are "sweet volumes," "nectar'd ambries of soul-feeding meats," "graceful quivers of love's dearest darts," "Cabinets of grace," "blazing comets," "living mir-

rors," "Bethlem cisterns," "pools of Hesebon, the
baths of grace," "turtle twins all bathed in virgin's
milk." The Infant Martyrs are lilies and roses, rubies
and pearls, the symbols of their innocence and their
blood. The verses on "Christ's Bloody Sweat," after
elaborately working out the figures of the olive press
and the wine press, conclude with the traditional
metaphors of the pelican and the phoenix, tokens of
the paradoxical union of fire and water. In Christ, the
phoenix's fire and the pelican's stream of blood are
united.

> He pelican's, he phoenix's fate doth prove,
>> Whome flames consume, whome streames en-
>> force to die;
> How burneth blood, how bleedeth burninge love,
>> Can one in flame and streame both bathe and
>> frye?

Paradox and oxymoron appear in verses like "I
Die Alive," which ring the rhetorical changes on the
mortality of the flesh and sin, the immortality of the
sanctified spirit.

> I live, but such a life as ever dies;
>> I die, but such a life as never ends;
> My death to end my dying life denies,
>> And life my loving death no whit amends.
> Thus still I die, yet still I do remain;
>> My living death by dying life is fed. . . .[51]

Giles Fletcher, whose *Christ's Victory and Triumph* (1610) remains a chief and charming ornament of English sacred poetry, is ordinarily thought of as a Spenserian, but his eye was not single. Writing in an eight-line stanza, adapted from that of the *Faerie Queene*, and reminiscent of Spenser in his personifications and allegories, his sensuous slowness of pace, and his delicacy and freshness of description, Fletcher frequently heightened his style with passages in the Italian manner, rhetorically florid, such as look toward Crashaw's most characteristic performances.

The poem opens with the familiar paradox of the Incarnation:

The birth of Him that no beginning knew,
    Yet gives beginning to all that are born;
And how the Infinite far greater grew
    By growing less; and how the rising morn,
That shot from heaven, did back to heaven
        return;
    The obsequies of Him that could not die,
And death of life, end of eternity,
How worthily He died, that died unworthily. . . .

With Renaissance generosity, Fletcher does not hesitate to adduce mythological analogies to sacred persons. Deucalion and Nisus are paired with Noah and Samson; Philomel types the Blessed Virgin weeping for her son; Christ as visitor to Hades is a later Orpheus; Christ ascending to Heaven, becomes the divine Ganymede.[52]

Fletcher lingers, sensuously, on the imagined loveliness of Christ's body:

> His cheeks as snowy apples sopped in wine,
> Had their red roses quenched with lilies white,
> And like to garden strawberries did shine,
> Washed in a bowl of milk, or rose-buds bright
> Unbosoming their breasts against the light. . . .

He celebrates the mystery of "delicious pain" experienced in mystic rapture:

> One of ten thousand souls I am, and more,
> That of His eyes, and their sweet wounds, complain:
> Sweet are the wounds of love—never so sore—
> Ah! might He often slay me so again!
> He never lives that thus is never slain.[53]

Fletcher was an Anglican, by no means an extreme High Churchman. Yet the baroque treatment of sacred themes is his as well as Southwell's.

Out of a sympathetic study of Southwell and Fletcher, Crashaw could, without question, have acquired the essentials of his final style: the antithesis, the oxymoron, the paradox, alliteration, homoioteleuton; sensuous metaphors for sensuous objects, the sensuous treatment of sacred themes. Assuredly, Crashaw must have read them both. But that in both

predecessors which was akin to Crashaw had come
to them from the Italian *concettists*. *St. Peter's Complaint* began as a translation of Tansillo's *Lacrime
di San Pietro;* its author, during his years in Rome,
acquired an aptitude for Spanish and Italian letters.[54]

A reader of *Steps to the Temple,* which provided,
as its longest piece, "Sospetto d'Herode, Libro
Primo," would, had he been Crashaw's contemporary,
have known that he was encountering, in English
version, the work of Giambattista Marino, the chief
Italian poet of the generation succeeding Tasso's.
Moving about from court to court, now at Turin,
now at Paris for eight years, as ward and adulator of
Marie de Medici, now at Rome, honored by Pope
Gregory XV, the ambitious, luxury-loving Neapoli-
tan made for himself, by the fecundity and brilliance
of his art, a vast reputation.[55] In his sketch of Italian
poetry, delivered in the schools, at Cambridge,
Joseph Beaumont, who did not mention Dante, reserved highest honors for Tasso; but Marino, "in
Epigrammate argutum, in Adonide heroicum, in In-
nocentibus splendidum, in singulis lauro dignum," [56]
held second place.

In spite of the allegorical interpretation supplied
by one of Marino's friends, *L'Adone* (1623) offers
an unmoral universe. Its twenty cantos extend to
more than heroic length, but its stature is not otherwise heroic: its slight "plot," requiring less than a
canto for its unfolding, is but pretext for the display
of a descriptive gift truly extraordinary, for pages

of sweetness which, were it not for the novelties and
metaphorical surprises tossed off by the wit, would
rapidly cloy. Indeed, for Beaumont, who was repelled by the loose secularity of *L'Adone*, the wonder
of Marino's achievement lay in its manner, such as to
make "Profaness almost seem *Divine*"; and the disparity between the inconsequential substance and the
splendor of style marked the triumph of Marino's
"vast wit." [57]

A nominal Catholic, and the protégé of Catholic
princes, Marino, as a matter of course, produced some
pious *madrigali* and a sacred epic, *La Strage degli
Innocenti* (1610); and it was this latter which, in
1637, Crashaw undertook to translate. The theme
of the Holy Innocents, those nameless and involun-
tary martyrs who died for Christ before His death,
permanently excited Crashaw's imagination. To it
he had awarded three of his *epigrammata*; and two
of the much sparser collection, the English epigrams,
paraphrase his own Latin.

> Goe smiling soules, your new built Cages breake,
> In heav'n you'l learne to sing ere here to speake,
> Nor let the milky fonts that bath your thirst,
> > Bee your delay;
> The place that calls you hence, is at the worst
> > Milke all the way.

Again, as though recollecting Prudentius' "flores
martyrum," he wrote:

> To see both blended in one flood
> The Mothers Milke, the childrens blood,
> Makes me doubt if Heaven will gather,
> *Roses* hence, or *Lillies* rather.[58]

The conceits in both of these epigrams may well
have come to Crashaw by way of Marino. In the
fourth book of the *Strage,* the Innocents are invoked
as both roses and lilies, and they mount to God's
bosom by the Milky Way.[59]

Marino's original comprises four books, of which
Crashaw translated but the first, the "Sospetto" or
"Suspicion of Herod." [60] This canto, not the most
likely to interest Crashaw, chiefly concerns Satan,
who, fallen from Heaven and hearing of God's
design to beget a son in time, visits Cruelty in her
arsenal of tortures, that she may stir up Herod to
kill the Infant God. The Second Book, devoted to
the long speeches made by the infernal peers in
council gathered, markedly suggests the second book
of *Paradise Lost,* but would hardly have lent itself
to Crashaw's style. Only in Books III and IV does
the poem reach its titular theme, the actual "Slaughter of the Innocents"; and these books offer so much
that was congenial to his temperament and his taste
that Crashaw, one must suppose, began his translation with full intention of completing it—that, indeed, he aimed chiefly at the brilliant finale of the
poem, which might well have exhibited his virtuosity
at its height.

It is not difficult, however, to conjecture why the translation remains incomplete. As it stands, it is much the longest of Crashaw's poems. An artist of the fancy, whose fecundity was of images, whose talent was for decoration, he lacked constructive and sustained power. Working verse by verse and stanza by stanza, he rarely envisaged a *whole* to which the parts should be subordinate. Doubtless the "Sospetto" cost Crashaw more labor than anything else he wrote; he rose ambitiously to its dimensions and produced, by emulation, an effect of largeness and strength which he was never to repeat.

A comparatively early work, the *Strage* exhibits less of the elaborate manner to which Marino has given his name than does the *Adone;* and, though the *Strage* does not lack rhetorical figures and conceits, it seems almost austere by comparison with Crashaw's paraphrase. Marino wrote in *ottava rima,* and Crashaw copies the stanza form; but the ampler dimensions of the English stanza offer him some latitude; and consistently he elaborates on his original. Marino's "Sospetto" has a certain ruggedness; Crashaw almost invariably softens and feminizes: his are the fine touches, the grace notes, the divisions, and the cadenzas.

Crashaw never attempts to translate Marino's words; instead, he recasts the substance of a passage, transmuting it into a texture which is not only English but Crashavian.

Marino's Italian for "in the eyes where gloom

lodges and death, there blazes a turbid and vermillion light" becomes:

> His eyes, the sullen dens of Death and Night,
> Startle the dull Ayre with a dismal red. . . .

Mestitia, which means gloom with overtones of sadness or grief, has been personified into Night, its symbolic equivalent. "Sullen dens," a figure suggested by Marino's *abberga* (lodges), has changed from verb to noun phrase, and grown pictorial. The Italian alliterates the pair *mestitia* and *morte*, the key words. Crashaw has not been able to master a suitable English parallel to Death; but he compensates by alliterating *Death* with *dens*, with *dull*, and with *dismal*, thereby doubling Marino's consonant sequence.[61] In the next stanza,

> Che la vista pestifera, e sanguigna,
> Con l'alito crudel, ch'avampa, e fuma,
> La pira accende horrible, e maligna,
> Che 'nconsumabilmente altrui consuma. . . .

is paraphrased:

> His flaming Eyes dire exhalation,
> Unto a dreadfull pile gives fiery Breath;
> Whose unconsum'd consumption preys upon
> The never-dying Life, of a long Death.

Marino's "unconsumabilmente . . . consuma" gives Crashaw an approximate English equivalent; but, for good measure, he adds another oxymoron unwarranted by his original.

The fifteenth stanza reads literally: "He [Herod] sees the silent shadow and the dusky horrors of that blessed, holy night struck and routed by the voices from Heaven and conquered by the angelic splendors. He sees farmers run, and shepherds run, through woods and wild caves, happy in bringing to the great Messiah the simple tribute of their rude gifts." There are two motifs in this stanza: heavenly light dispelling the darkness which reigned at Christ's birth; and the gift-bearing shepherds hastening to Bethlehem. Crashaw apprehends these concepts, but develops them in his own far more elaborate style.

> Hee saw how in that blest Day-bearing Night,
> The Heav'n-rebuked shades made hast away;
> How bright a Dawne of Angels with new light
> Amaz'd the midnight world, and made a Day
> Of which the Morning knew not: Mad with spight
> Hee markt how the poore Shepheards ran to pay
> Their simple Tribute to the Babe, whose Birth
> Was the great businesse both of Heav'n and
> Earth.

In comparison Marino seems thin. The paradox of "Day-bearing Night"; the substitution of the brilliantly metaphorical "Dawne" for the abstraction, "splendors"; the strong juxtaposition, "midnight world"; the conceit on Day and Morning; the final couplet, with its alliteration of three emphatic words

—in short, the striking figures and phrases—are all
of Crashaw's devising.

Many of the best lines have little or no pretext.
From the hint, "spiantar da le radici il Mondo,"
Crashaw writes, "And crush the world *till his wide
corners meet*." "You of whose brave worth,/The
frighted stars tooke fainte experience" is entirely
his; so is "Bathing their hot limbs in life's pretious
flood." From "eterno mele" he draws "Immortall
Hony for the Hive of Loves." The abstract "onde
memoria al mondo resti" is prose statement; with
double personification and double alliteration Crashaw transmutes it into "Thy Fames full noise, makes
proud the patient Earth. . . ." Marino has only to
mention the "illustrious band of three wise heroes
from the East"; Crashaw introduces a hierarchical
distinction and appends a paradox:

> Three Kings (or what is more) three Wise men
> went
> Westward to find the worlds true *Orient*.[62]

Marino displays his own resources chiefly in Book
IV, in which Herod's young son is, for dramatic
irony, killed, his queen commits suicide, and the
Innocents' souls are welcomed to Limbo by the
canorous David. He accumulates oxymora: dearest
sighs and groans, sweetest pain, most lovely death.
He puns: "O stille, o sangue, o *stille*, no, ma *stelle*"
(not drops of blood but stars). He analogizes:

Herod's queen and her son, lying in their own gore,
are rocks of marble in a crimson sea (scogli di *marmo*
in *mar* vermiglio). He personifies boldly: the Sun,
sinking at the end of the slaughter, is ambitious to
empurple himself in so beautiful a sea of blood.[63]

In his love poetry, he was especially renowned for
his metaphors, his *concetti*—the kisses which become
a medicine, a trumpet, a combat; the mouth which is
sweet warrior, an agreeable prison, a living death, a
jail of pearls, and an urn of gems.[64]

The Elizabethans, following the Renaissance Italians, had exhausted the obvious comparisons and the
milder hyperboles—eyes like the sun, cheeks like
roses, lips like coral, breath like perfume, breasts
like snow. From this outworn stock, both Donne and
Marino turned away with distaste, but in separate
directions—Donne to geometry, Marino to jewelry.
Donne illustrates the palpable by the impalpable, or
one kind of impalpable by another, also impalpable;
he draws upon commerce, science, law, theology for
metaphors unexploited by the less learned and the
less versatile. Marino—in this respect like the
Petrarchans—still chiefly analogizes within the scope
of the palpable, illustrating things by other things—
nature's creations by man's artifacts, one sense perception in terms drawn from another sense; he depends upon his undeniable "wit" to provide fresh
thrills wrested from more or less familiar objects,
by oddly juxtaposing them, or by developing each of
the juxtaposed terms until the strain of the imagina-

tive distance between them is felt at least as power-fully as the force of the analogy.

Crashaw's exhibition piece in the manner of Marino is not the "Suspicion of Herod" but "The Weeper," written a few years earlier, but obviously under the conjoint influence of the Jesuit poets and Marino; and the English poet did not hesitate to borrow as well as to put at interest what he borrowed.

The theme, the love and penitence of the Magdalen, compliantly lent itself to stylization. Tears are the obvious symbol, as they are the effect, of grief; the obvious symbol for passion is flame: fire and water, two elements, become correspondences of psychological "elements." Concettist treatment of the Magdalen naturally centers upon these and their analogical developments.

The paradoxical proximity of water and fire had occasioned the epigram of Biderman on the saints, Mary Magdalen and Afra, painted on a single canvas —the one with her tears, the other with her flames. But the paradox is the greater when, in one and the same person, there dwell together, tears and flames, fire and water. In the ardent penitent, neither ele-ment, as in Nature, extinguishes the other, for love prompts the contrition: the more one loves, the more one weeps for having sinned against the beloved. Flames, instead of quelling, increase the flow of tears; the water makes the fire burn more brightly.[65]

The conceit is announced in the opening couplet prefixed to Crashaw's "The Weeper."

Loe where a Wounded Heart with Bleeding Eyes
  conspire
Is she a Flaming Fountain, or a Weeping fire! [66]

The poem may best be described as a free fantasia,
a theme with variations. Crashaw might have afforded it structure by utilizing the story of the
Magdalen as told in the *Golden Legend* and as
rehearsed and expanded by the poets, or by taking
the penitent sinner as theme for meditation. He does
neither. Nor is Crashaw concerned to analyze the
character of Mary or the nature of her conversion
from sinner to saint or to delineate her revulsion
from sin and her new-found faith. From his poem,
Crashaw has excluded the story, the character, the
psychology, and the moral. Mary has no part in her
poem; it should be called not "The Weeper," but
"Tears." And indeed there is no real distinction
between this dithyramb and "The Teare" which
followed it in *Steps to the Temple.* In revision of
the longer poem, Crashaw borrows a stanza from the
shorter, evidently its predecessor and first draft; but
he might have subsumed it all within his flexible
form.

The original version of "The Weeper" runs to
twenty-three stanzas. The charge that each of these
divisions begins afresh is extravagant: frequently a
metaphor lingers. Mary's eyes stay stars for two
stanzas; for another pair, they are jewels; two
stanzas celebrate the rivalry between tears and bal-

sam; another two make the tears the measure of time; three stanzas sequentially trace the tears as they flow, miraculously, upward, to serve the cherubs of Heaven as breakfast cream and the angels as wine; the final three are united as questions and answer.

But aside from the invocatory first stanza and the rhetorical dialogue of the last three, the sections might, imperceptibly, change places. The poem is a series of metaphors, in which the poet perpetually returns to his initial image—tears. It is a theme with variations—only the variations lack much variety: they do not change timbre or increase in resonance; and though they are all ingenious, even their ingenuity is not climactic.

The consequence is a poem in which the sweetness vastly predominates over the sadness, a poem so confectionary that we almost forget that these are tears and mistake them for *bonbons*. Not only has the penitent sinner disappeared, but the tears as effects of contrition, as symbols of penitence—as, in short, anything more than round objects capable of infinite iridescence—have vanished with her.

In the second edition of *Steps*, published two years later, "The Weeper" has been extended to thirty-one stanzas. Crashaw's impulse was ever to dilate, to display further ingenuity. Whatever changes in arrangement have been made, work, however, toward a less staccato, a more sequential, effect. He now succeeds, through four stanzas, in keeping to variations of a single conceit—the strife between the sunny

cheeks and the raining eyes of the Magdalen. In the
new version appears first the celebrated transmuta-
tion of tears into "walking baths," "portable, and
compendious oceans." But this no whit exceeds in
grotesqueness the earlier (and retained) picture of
Mary's tears, turned cream, become the cherub's
breakfast.[67]

The same Marinistic method Crashaw applied, in a
poem apparently written at about the same time as
"The Weeper," to the wounds of the crucified Christ.
Are the wounds eyes or mouths? Both.

> Lo! a mouth, whose full-bloom'd lips
>   At too deare a rate are roses.
> Lo! a blood-shot eye! that weeps
>   And many a cruell teare discloses.
>
> O thou that on this foot hast laid
>   Many a kisse, and many a Teare,
> Now thou shal't have all repaid,
>   Whatsoe're thy charges were.
>
> This foot hath got a Mouth and lippes,
>   To pay the sweet summe of thy kisses:
> To pay thy Teares, an Eye that weeps
>   In stead of Teares such Gems as this is.
>
> The difference onely this appeares,
>   (Nor can the change offend)
> The debt is paid in *Ruby*-Teares,
>   Which thou in Pearles did'st lend.[68]

The wounds, like the Magdalen's tears, are abstracted from their psychological context and, viewed as objects of sense perception, find metaphorical counterparts in other equally palpable things.

Even more than the emblem-like grotesqueness of the "blood-shot eye," it is this externality which has repelled many readers, including old-fashioned Evangelicals accustomed to sing of the "fountain filled with blood drawn from Immanuel's veins." Cowper's sanguinary hymn, like others of its sort, celebrates the Atonement and attempts, by visualization of Christ's passion, to arouse to penitence those sinners who, once "plunged beneath that flood," will lose their guilty stains; but the emphasis is at once doctrinal and hortatory; the Crucifixion is viewed in the light of its consequence to mankind.

For Crashaw, on the other hand, this would have seemed too subjective, too self-centered, almost, one might say, too calculating an attitude. Doubtless Christ's blood was shed as a ransom for many; gratitude for benefits, however, is not piety. In Himself, as God and as Man, Christ invites supreme adoration.

Not its manner but its morals, its subject, constituted, for Beaumont and Crashaw, what was vicious in *L'Adone*. The bodies and loves of sinners do not merit such expenditure of wit. But eloquence and ingenuity befit the laud of earthly potentates and, still more, that of the saints. Then in addressing the King of Kings, hyperbole cannot, rightly, be said to exist, and the only degree of comparison is the superlative. The dedication page of Beaumont's *Psyche* bears, thus, the following inscription: "Into the most Sacred Treasury of the Praise and the Glory of Incarnate God, the world's most merciful RE-DEEMER, the unworthiest of His Majesties creatures, in all possible prostrate veneration, begs leave to cast this his dedicated mite."

For Southwell, Fletcher, Beaumont, and Crashaw, the sensuous celebration of saints and Christ had, substantially, a Catholic logic. By the incarnational principle, the soul imprints character upon the body; the user imparts virtue to the instrument; the final cause, operating through subsidiary causes, bestows its value upon them. Again, if the whole be supremely great, then all its parts and accouterments must have supremacy in kind. The body of a saint thus gains power through its cohabitation with the sanctified soul; and, in every least relic of the body, some of this power inheres. Of all human bodies, Christ's must necessarily be supreme in worth; if, as Marvell playfully grants to his "coy mistress," millennia alone could accommodate her adequate praise, then even eternity could scarcely suffice to celebrate the form which vested the most high God.

> Stretch all thy powres; call if you can
> Harpes of heavn to hands of man.
> This soveraign subject sitts above
> The best ambition of thy love.[69]

The Marinistic method, when applied to sacred subjects, was perfectly conformable to the principles of the Counter-Reformation. From the logic which prompted poems like "The Weeper" and "The Wounds" Crashaw never seceded; but those two poems represent the most unmitigated practice of the method. In the work of his maturity, the method, mastered, becomes a resource, flexible to the purposes of its user.

4. CATHOLIC THEMES AND ATTITUDES

CRASHAW's poetic development must not be conceived as disjunct from his spiritual. Indeed, there is inevitable a crudeness in a criticism which disserts now of substance and now of form. In a writer of any integrity, mode of vision and rhetorical method are but the inner and outer aspects, the soul and body, of a single experience; and a man's experimental years may be described almost indifferently as "finding himself" or finding his style. So naturalism means ambiguously a philosophy and an aesthetic; so symbolism is composition in percepts intimating concepts and, inwardly, an attitude which regards the real as both immaterial and yet expressible only through its correspondential appearances to the senses.

Practically, it is convenient to disengage the subjects which excite the mind of a poet, the things he is said to "write about"; and to talk of his subjects need not and should not imply that the meaning of a

poem is equivalent to its paraphrase in prose, still less
to that kind of topic which can be listed in an index.
To say that a poem is "patriotic" or "religious" is to
tell us nothing of its poetic method or value; but it
does tell us something about the mind of the poet,
the character of which makes poetry not good or bad
but small or large.

Crashaw's religious poetry was composed in an
ideological as well as a literary context; and, for the
reconstruction of what his poems meant to him and
to some at least of his seventeenth-century readers,
it is necessary to contemplate the devotions, the art,
and the belles-lettres of the Counter-Reformation,
the import of its heroes, the popularity of its cults,
the *données* upon which Crashaw worked. The Magdalen, St. Alexis, St. Teresa; nuptial mysticism and
the mysticism of the *via negativa;* and the hymns of
the medieval Church are so many cults, traditions,
données which engaged the attention of Crashaw;
and to consider what they were in themselves and for
the age, what drew Crashaw to them and what he
made of them is to advance one's apprehension of the
poet's development and to supply that knowledge of
what the seventeenth-century poet could have meant
which should control, though not restrict, the meaning of his poetry for a later day.

In its devotional life, and in its ecclesiastically
directed art, the Counter-Reformation systematically
fostered those doctrines and practices which Protestantism had rejected. Among these practices was the

sacrament of penance; among these doctrines, the belief that man might fall from grace and yet, by his contrition, win ultimate peace and glory. The two illustrious sinner-saints whom Bellarmine cited in his *Disputations* were St. Peter and St. Mary Magdalen; and both of these became the themes for innumerable poems and paintings.[70]

In the Gospels, the Magdalen is thrice mentioned —as a woman out of whom Christ cast seven devils, as present at the Crucifixion, and as the first to whom the risen Lord appeared; but the Western Church presently identified her with Mary, the sister of Martha and Lazarus, and with the unnamed penitent who brought an alabaster box of ointment and, with her tears, washed Christ's feet, wiping them with her hair.

French tradition continues the story: After the Ascension, Mary, Martha, Lazarus, and others were set adrift in a boat without sails, oars, or rudder, but, divinely conducted, they made a safe passage to the shores of Provence. Having first converted the pagans of the land by her preaching and her miracles, the Magdalen retired to a grotto in a barren wilderness, where, during thirty years, she devoted herself to penance for her past sins. The angels visited her at the canonical hours, carrying her in their arms to heights from which she could hear the celestial harmonies and see "what eye hath not seen"; and in her solitude, surrounded by angels, she died.[71]

In the seventeenth century, the Provençal legend

was still accepted; and the Magdalen, who has been called the century's favorite heroine, was generally represented—by painters like Guerchino, Ribera, the Caracci, Rubens, and Van Dyke—in the solitude of her grotto, where, alabaster box in hand, she meditates. She was equally a subject for the Catholic poets, whether they wrote in Latin, Italian, French, or English.

A Jesuit, Cabilliavus, published in 1625 a collection of some hundred and seventy Latin poems, called *Magdalena,* and treating the Biblical account, the legend, and the theme from every possible point of view. A few titles will illustrate the method: Divine Love wounds the Magdalen with a fiery weapon; the Magdalen in washing Christ's feet washes herself; the Magdalen satiates her thirst with tears; dying, she is turned into a fountain; Love prepares for navigation in the Magdalen's tears; the Magdalen, voyaging to Heaven, weaves a sail from her tresses. Her tears are likened to jewels, stars, an ocean; she suffers shipwreck in the floods of her own penitence. Of Latin epigrams on the Saint, Remond's "De Lacrymis S. Mariae Magdalenae" and those by John Owen and Marius Bettinus [72] were certainly familiar to Crashaw.

Marino has three madrigals on the Magdalen. In French, César de Nostre-Dame, Durant, Remy de Beauvais, and Le Clerc wrote "heroic" poems.[73] English Catholics, too, offered their devotions. Robert Southwell's moving *Mary Magdalene's Teares*

(1591) took the form of rhetorical prose: "But not finding the favour, to accompany him in death, and loathing after him to remain in life, the fire of her true affection inflamed her hart, and her inflamed hart resolved into incessant teares: so that burning and bathing between love and griefe, she led a life ever dying, and felt a death never ending." An eloquent poem, bearing the same title as Southwell's prose, and attributed to Gervase Markham, appeared in 1601; in 1603, *Saint Marie's Magdalen's Conversion*, by J. C.; in 1604, an anonymous poem, *Mary Magdalens Seven Lamentations*; in 1617, the Jesuit Sweetnam's *Saint Mary Magdalens Pilgrimage to Paradise*, combining legendary biography with meditations, prose, and verse.[74]

"The Weeper" is not, then, a unique piece, as, presented in English anthologies, it sometimes seems. It is a poem on a theme much celebrated, in its day, by Catholics and Continentals; and it is a poem conscious of its ancestral heirlooms, out of which it assembles and repolishes all manner of metaphorical jewels.

Crashaw's three "Alexias" elegies paraphrased and developed passages from a set of seven Latin elegies, "Uxoris Sancti Alexii Querimoniae," by the Jesuit Father, Francis Remond.[75] But Remond, writing a Christian counterpart to one of Ovid's *Heroides*, did not invent his heroine or the strange husband who occasioned her strange plight. There are fashions in saints as well as in matters more mundane, and St.

Alexis has been superseded by the Little Flower;
but, from the thirteenth century to the end of the
seventeenth, his devotion seems to have enjoyed great
popularity; and his life inspired many narrative
poems and ballads. A canticle, written by Père de
Barry and dedicated to the pupils of the Ursulines,
puts upon the lips of a seventeenth-century school-
girl:

> Alexis formerly
> Was saint of saints for me
> For Alexis my heart aye sighed
> For Alexis my spirit cried. . . .[76]

Alexis, reputed to have lived in the fifth century,
during the reign of the Emperors Arcadius and
Honorius, was the only son of a long-childless couple,
Roman nobles of wealth and virtue. From his earliest
years, he was humble, charitable, and devoted to God,
to Whose service he vowed himself; and, though he
donned the silk and gold garments suitable to his
station, he wore haircloth next his skin and, com-
plaisant in public, spent his private hours in mortifica-
tions. When he attained a marriageable age, the
parents provided for him a king's daughter: to obey
his parents, he married her; but, on his marriage
night, to obey God, he secretly escaped from his wife
and parents, journeyed to the Far East, and, for
seventeen years, lived incognito, begging alms at the
church porch. At the end of that time, a statue of the

Blessed Virgin cried out, "Seek the Man of God."
Discovered, and about to be reverenced by the popu-
lace, the humble Alexis fled back to Rome and, con-
cealing his identity, besought shelter from his still
disconsolate parents and wife. Taken in, he lived in
his own palace for another seventeen years, was
housed in a den under the marble steps, was fed upon
crusts and scraps from the table, was mocked and
despised by the servants. At length, a mysterious
voice cried, "Seek the Man of God"; and the Em-
peror and the Pope, followed by the people, sought
and discovered the saint's retreat. He lay dead, holding in his hand a parchment upon which, with his last
strength, he had written the story of his life. His
parents and his wife burst into tears; and the holy
body was removed to the basilica of St. Peter's,
where the Pope said a solemn requiem.[77]

The moral of this strange legend seems that of
sacrificing the natural affections and the normal com-
forts to the glory of God. We recall Christ's words,
"He that loveth father or mother more than me is
not worthy of me," and the invitation to the parabolic
marriage feast, rejected by one of the bidden guests
in the words, "I have married a wife, and therefore I
cannot come." In order to make the antithesis the
sharper, the saint's motivation is narrowed. His parents and his wife are good Christians; and, according
to Remond—and Crashaw—the forsaken wife is
willing to live with him in complete abstinence from
the pleasures of the bed.

If Heates of holyer love and high desire
Make bigge thy fair brest with immortall fire,
What needes my virgin lord fly thus from me,
Who only wish his virgin wife to be?
Wittnesse, chast heavns! no happyer vowes I know
Than to a virgin Grave untouch't to goe.[78]

The saint suffers a voluntary martyrdom of poverty
and contumely; his parents and his wife, who laments
throughout the elegies, suffer also, and less meritori-
ously.

A third of Crashaw's themes was St. Teresa. The
sixteenth-century Spanish mystic received beatifica-
tion in 1610; the following year, her autobiography
was translated into English. She was canonized in
1622; and this event was likewise commemorated by
an English translation of the *Vida*, said to have been
done by Toby Matthew.

One of the extraordinary women of all time, the
saint coupled in herself the rôles of Mary and
Martha. As founder and superior of the Discalced
Carmelites, she exhibited marked capacities for or-
ganization and administration; as ruler of her convent and counselor of her nuns, she was sensible,
shrewd, humorous, realistic. She experienced levitations, trances, raptures, saw visions. At the bidding of
her director, she wrote eight books, of which the most
celebrated, *The Way of Perfection* and *The Interior
Castle*, guide the ascent of souls from normal piety to
special and supernatural graces.[79]

Her fame traversed Europe. Her books were translated into Latin, French, Italian, Flemish, German, and Polish as well as English. The arts commemorated her visions and ecstasies.[80]

In the most celebrated of her visions, she saw, as she records in her *Life*, a seraph holding in his hand a fire-tipped dart of gold, which he thrust several times through the heart of the saint. "The paine of it," she says, "was so excessive, that it forced me to utter those groanes; and the suavitie, which that extremitie of paine gave, was also so very excessive, that there was no desiring at all, to be ridd of it. . . ."[81]

It is this celebrated "transverberation" which Bernini translated into flowing, undulating marble. The barefooted saint, floating among clouds, but with one foot swinging free from even this security, falls back in a swoon, her mouth agape, her eyes almost shut. The face is relaxed; but rapture speaks in the writhing swirl of her garments and the tumult of folds. To her left stands the winged seraph, bearing his golden wand and ready to inflict the sweet pain of love's wound.

Of Crashaw's three poems on the great mystic, the first, "In Memory of the Vertuous and Learned Lady *Madre de* Teresa," may have been written as early as 1638. This and the second of the trio, "An Apologie," made their initial appearance in *Steps to the Temple* (1646) and were reprinted in 1648 with the addition of a third, "The Flaming Heart: Upon the booke and picture of Teresa, as she is usually expressed with a

Seraphim beside her," which is likely to have been written in Paris.

"The Flaming Heart," which takes its title from Matthew's translation of the saint's life—reissued in 1642 with a dedication to Queen Henrietta Maria—is for the most part a work of unfired ingenuity, occasioned by a picture of the saint's transverberation. The saint is depicted as passive; the seraph, as active: quite *natural*; but the paradox is that "Love's Passives are his activ'st part," and the saint incomparably more vigorous than any rosy-cheeked and inexperienced seraph. On the theme Crashaw works many rather arid variations. This shrinking female is surely "some weak, inferiour, woman saint," not the great Teresa. The reader is bidden to reverse the picture, and reverse the sexes of the participants; for Teresa was "for masculine courage of performance more than a woman." His should be the blushes, hers the fires; his the veil, hers the dart; for Teresa and her mystical writings have pierced more hearts than did ever seraph.

After sixty-eight lines of such exercises, Crashaw's mood changes. He becomes impassioned and eloquent as he contemplates the triumphant progress of Teresa and the "conquering leaves of her books," her sequent train of converts and devotees.

> Let this immortall life wherere it comes
> Walk in a crowd of loves and *Martyrdomes.*
> Let mystick *Deaths* wait on't; and wise soules be
> The love-slain witnesses of this life of thee.

Here the poem ended in the version of 1648; in 1652, it was lengthened twenty-four lines by the addition of an invocation to the saint, probably the best-known passage in all Crashaw's work. Till now, the poet has been detached, seeing the saint thronged by her captive souls, but not specifically incorporating himself in their number. Now, in his own person, he addresses the saint.

> O sweet incendiary! shew here thy art,
> Upon this carcasse of a hard, cold, hart,
> Let all thy scatter'd shafts of light, that play
> Among the leaves of my larg Books of day,
> Combin'd against this *Brest* at once break in
> And take away from me my self and sin. . . .

The persistent and moving parallelism of the conclusion forms a Litany; as an Anglican, Crashaw must have heard its rhythm in the cadences of the Prayer Book: "By thine Agony and Bloody Sweat; by thy Cross and Passion; by thy precious Death and Burial; by thy glorious Resurrection and Ascension. . . ."[82]

> By all thy dowr of *Lights* and *Fires;*
> By all the eagle in thee, all the dove;
> By all thy lives and deaths of love;
> By thy larg draughts of intellectuall day,
> And by thy thirsts of love more large than they;
> By all thy brim-fill'd Bowles of feirce desire
> By thy last Morning's draught of liquid fire;

By the full kingdom of that finall kisse
That seiz'd thy parting Soul, and seal'd thee
   his . . .
By all of *Him* we have in *Thee;*
Leave nothing of my *Self* in me.
Let me so read thy life, that I
Unto all life of mine may dy.

There is no passage in the "Hymne" so magnificent as this; but, as a poem, the "Hymne" is much the best of the trio: it has a unity and sequence, a flow and a crescendo which Crashaw was rarely able to contrive. The title, "In Memory of the Vertuous and Learned Lady *Madre de* Teresa, that sought an early Martyrdome," sounds the central and persistent *theme:* Martyrdom. Love is "Absolute sole Lord" of life—and death.

Teresa is chiefly to be celebrated as "Love's Martyr," *Charitatis Victima.* The opening narration, based upon an early episode of the *Vida,* concerns her childhood escapade.[88] At six, she ran away from home in order to convert the Moors. If her words might not convince, then at least her blood could convert them: fired with pious ambition, she sought the crown of martyrdom. The second section displays the character of her mature spirituality. God at once denied and fulfilled her juvenile ambition; for not her death but her life was to constitute her martyrdom, and her executioners were to be not Saracens but seraphim.

The mystical experience—on this, all its practi-

tioners and exegetes agree—commingles pain and joy.
But particularly is this true of what they call the
"wound of love"; and Crashaw's poem is dominated
by this state, described so eloquently by St. Teresa, St.
John of the Cross, and St. Francis of Sales. In it, God
pierces the soul with such darts of fire that pain and
joy are simultaneous and of equal strength: joy, because God loves the soul and longs for it and visits
it; pain, because the soul cannot love God as he deserves, because God's visitations are temporary, because the body cannot endure the strain put upon it
by rapture, because the soul longs for death and perfect union with its Spouse.[84]

A fusion in equal intensity of pain and joy: a
special figure, the oxymoron, rhetorically corresponds
to the *wound of love* and is the almost inevitable expression of it, as the paradox is the almost inevitable
expression of the Incarnation. St. Francis of Sales in
his *Traité de l'Amour de Dieu*, which was translated
by Crashaw's friend, Carre, compares the wound of
love to the juice of pomegranates, "so compounded
of sweete and sour, that one can hardly discerne,
whether it delights the taste more by its sweetish
tarteness or tarte sweetness." St. John of the Cross
apostrophizes: "O delicious wound, then, and the
more delicious the more the cautery of love penetrates the inmost substance of the soul, burning
all it can burn that it may supply all the delight it
can give"; the soul, says St. Teresa, "is conscious of
having received a delicious wound, but cannot dis-

cover how, nor who gave it, yet recognizes it as a most precious grace, and hopes the hurt will never heal." [85] The mystic suffers excruciating pains in the spirit and sometimes in the body; yet, so far from wishing release from his suffering, he prays God to continue it, to wound him yet more deeply.

This is the state which colors Crashaw's poem. He writes of a "sweet and subtle Pain," of "intolerable Joyes," of the "sweetly-killing Dart," of "delicious Wounds, that weep Balsam to heal themselves with."

The "death more mystical and high" of the "Hymne" is the consequence of successive *wounds* made by the flame of Divine Love. The death of the body is common to all; but the death of the soul, the *mors angelorum*, is the high privilege of the elect whom God has chosen to wound and inflame till they are all one wound, one flame. According to St. John, the "Divine cautery of love heals the wound which love has caused, and by each application renders it greater. The healing which love brings is to wound again what was wounded before, until the soul melts away in the fire of love. So when the soul shall become wholly one wound of love it will then be transformed in love, wounded with love."

> Thus
> When These thy *Deaths*, so numerous
> Shall all at last dy into one,
> And melt thy Soul's sweet mansion;
> Like a soft lump of incense, hasted

By too hott a fire, and wasted
Into perfuming clouds, so fast
Shalt thou exhale to Heaven at last
In a resolving *Sigh*. . . .

The concluding section of the "Hymne" sees
Teresa received into Heaven, welcomed by the Lord
and His Mother, greeted by her old friends, the
angels, who—Crashaw says with a passing homeli-
ness—are "glad at their own home now" to entertain
her. Her state is seraphical; her joy, permanent and
unmixed. Yet even in Paradise she bears the marks,
transfigured as they are, of her spiritual martyrdom:
her "paines sitt bright" upon her; her wounds
"blush." Meanwhile all around her crowd her converts, the crowned souls who form the stars in her
crown, the fruits of her virginal union with the
Heavenly Bridegroom.

In the "Hymne," one of Crashaw's four or five
best pieces, he unites two themes intensely dear to
him—martyrdom and mysticism; in this poem, indeed, the two themes grow one: to live the mystical
life is to die, not in a moment, but throughout a life
—to die, at the hand not of an enemy but of a lover.

These poems, particularly the "Hymne," flow with
a passionate ease almost unparalleled in Crashaw's
work. The metaphors are less crowded and developed
at greater length. They are not ornamental, as in
"The Weeper," but structural.

Though Crashaw has often been called a mystical

poet, only five or six of his poems (the Teresan cycle, "Prayer," and "To the Same Party: Councel concerning her Choice") give strict warrant for such claim; and in "Prayer" alone he offers a generalized version of what he understands the mystical experience to be. Of mystical writers, Crashaw cites, apart from St. Teresa, only the Christian Neo-Platonist who assumed the name of Dionysius the Areopagite,[86] though he must have also known at least St. Augustine, St. Bernard, and that great Catholic rhetorician with whose spirit and style he had so much affinity, St. Francis of Sales.

Among the mystics, two types differentiate themselves: the philosophically minded, usually, though not invariably, in the Neo-Platonic tradition—St. Augustine, the pseudo-Dionysius, Meister Eckhart, the author of the *Cloud of Unknowing*, St. John of the Cross; and the imagistically minded, given to trances and visions—Suso, St. Catherine of Siena, St. Teresa. The first of these types pursues the *via negativa:* God, it holds, so transcends as really to be unlike any created thing; and we reach Him by voiding our memories and fancies of images derived from sense perception. The second type never forsakes its picture-thinking, its symbols, drawn principally from human love and human marriage. For one, God is "best known not defining Him," "a deep and dazzling darkness";[87] for the other, He is the Heavenly Archer, the Ravisher, the Bridegroom.

Crashaw's ode on the Epiphany explores the mysti-

cism of the *via negativa*. Though partly Marinist in
its figures, it, more than any of his other poems, seems
metaphysical in style and intent; the absence from it
of sensuous imagery, including visual, differentiates
it from his habitual manner. Like so much of his work,
it builds upon paradox, but its particular paradox is
less provable to the finger tips, drier, more abstract,
as befits the doctrine which it symbolizes.

In spite of particular obscurities, the central theme
of the "Epiphanie" is clear; and, when once one
grasps the connection between what at first sight seem
unrelated episodes, the whole exhibits a logic of development beyond Crashaw's wont. Fundamental to
the poem is a contrast of natural and supernatural
light, expressed in an antithesis between the sun of
the heavens and the Heavenly Sun, the Creator of
the solar system; this bodies forth in parable the
antithesis between pagan cults and Christianity, and
between the "wisdom of this world" and that higher
wisdom which, to the senses and to the "rational
mind," seems foolishness.

The contrast is no mere device of philosophic or
poetic fancy. The winter solstice occurs on December
22; on the twenty-fifth, the Romans and other pagans
celebrated the birthday of the sun. Furthermore, solar
worship was common throughout the Orient, especially among the Babylonians, Assyrians, the Persian
devotees of Mithra, and the Egyptians; and many
religions, alien by inception, became, through syn-
cretism, interpreted as solar.[88] Of these deities and

religions, Crashaw specifically mentions Osiris and Mithra, the Egyptian and the Persian. Partly, no doubt, because of the scriptural allusions to the "wisdom of the Egyptians," partly because of the Renaissance vogue of the hieroglyphics, supposed to conceal, in emblematic form, some occult spirituality, he seems, in this poem, chiefly to connect the magi with Egypt; and their religion is called a "more specious mist" than its rivals.

According to the synoptic Evangelists, the sun actually did homage to its Maker: for three hours, during the Crucifixion, an eclipse darkened the earth; and this fact of Gospel history is, in Crashaw's ode, prophesied by the Magi attending the Nativity.[89]

That forfeiture of noon to night shall pay
All the idolatrous thefts done by this night of
    day;
And the Great Penitent presse his own pale lipps
With an elaborate love-eclipse
    To which the low world's lawes
    Shall lend no cause
Save those domestick which he borrowes
From our sins and his own sorrowes.

By its eclipse, for which "natural law" offers no explanation, the sun does penance for having so long accepted illicit worship and signifies its shame at a corrupt humanity which can allow its Saviour to die.

"The eclipse of the sun is when it is new moon; the eclipse of the moon when 'tis full. They say Dionysius

was so converted by the eclipse that happened at our
Saviour's death, because it was neither of these, and
so could not be natural." [90] The worthy thus alluded
to in Selden's *Table Talk* was a fifth-century Syrian
monk, who, deeply versed in the Neo-Platonism of
Plotinus and Proclus, wrote mystical treatises bearing, for honorific purposes, the name of Dionysius the
Areopagite, Athenian disciple of St. Paul.[91] "Dionysius" taught that the return of the soul to God is effected by successive denials and abstractions: the
initiate "must leave behind *all* things both in the
sensible and in the intelligible worlds, till he enters
into the darkness of nescience that is truly mystical,"
the "Divine darkness" which surrounds God, "the
absolute No-thing which is above all existence" and
all reason.[92] Crashaw connected the manner of Dionysius' conversion with the doctrine of the *via negativa*.

> Thus shall that reverend child of light,
> By being scholler first of that new night,
> Come forth Great master of the mystick day;
> And teach obscure *Mankind* a more close way
> By the frugall negative light
> Of a most wise and well-abused Night . . .
> Now by abased liddes shall [we] learn to be
> Eagles; and shutt our eyes that we may see.

Thus the argument of the ode develops: the sun
worshipers come west to find their East, discover in
the terrestrial night their heavenly day, foresee that

eclipse of the sun which betokens the submission of the natural to the supernatural; this same eclipse converted Dionysius, who expounded the miracle in his doctrine that the denial of sensuous experience opens the vision to spiritual illumination.

The relation between this poem and its companion piece on the Nativity is one to invite speculation. The latter contemplates the Child Jesus sleeping between the pure yet warm breasts of His Mother; the former contemplates the God of the philosophers, the Logos, the *Lumen de Lumine*. Were the two attitudes, the corresponding two styles, designed as dramatic characterizations; or does the second ode represent some attempted and never consummated change in the character of Crashaw's religious life and his poetic method? Of the two types of mystics, the visionaries and the philosophers, Crashaw's temperament markedly allied him with the former; and the *via negativa*, with its denial of sensuous analogies, runs counter to the baroque belief that in my flesh shall I see God in His flesh. Whether, therefore, as experiment or imaginative projection of an attempt to impose upon one temperament the method natural to another, the ode on the Epiphany stands apart and alone in Crashaw's work.

In addition to these poems on the saints and the mystics, Crashaw applied himself, possibly at the suggestion of Thomas Carre, to the paraphrase of medieval Latin hymns. The 1648 edition of *Steps*, in which these versions first appeared, attempted, for

the propitiation of Protestant scruples, to disguise
their provenience and character under such general
titles as "A Hymn to our Savior by the Faithfull Re-
ceiver of the Sacrament," a "Hymn in meditation of
the Day of Judgment," and "Upon our B. Saviours
Passion." These three—as *Carmen Deo Nostro,*
published at Paris by the printer to the Archbishop,
first avowed—had, as their respective originals,
"Adoro Te," by St. Thomas Aquinas, Thomas of
Celano's "Dies Irae," and the Office of the Holy
Cross, to be found in medieval Books of the Hours
and in such Sarum primers as appeared during the
reign of Mary Tudor.[93] The 1648 volume included,
also, Crashavian versions of a second Eucharistic
hymn by Aquinas, "Lauda Sion Salvatorem,"[94] of
Fortunatus' "Vexilla Regis," of the medieval hymn
to the Blessed Virgin, "O Gloriosa Domina," and of
da Todi's "Stabat Mater."

Crashaw must have known them before his submission to Rome; but there would be, thereafter, a particular appeal in these hymns, to which, before the
Wesleys, the English Church had no equivalent—
and a particular fitness in his translating them, by the
act joining his individual talent to the choir of Catholic poetry. His versions were, in effect, moderniza-
tions such as Dryden performed upon passages from
Chaucer, and Pope upon two of Donne's satires; they
took venerable themes and harmonized them afresh
in the style of a later age.

To "Sancta Maria," Crashaw prefixed the explanatory subtitle, "A Pathetical Descant upon the Devout Plainsong of Stabat Mater Dolorosa": the same rubric might have done service for all of the group. Plainsong, the traditional music of the Church, offers, like the music of the Greeks, melody alone, and that written in the ecclesiastical modes which preceded the major and minor keys. By its austerity, unaccompanied plainsong better suited the monastic offices than it did the congregational mass; and, from the twelfth century until the end of the sixteenth, when the polyphony of Palestrina and Byrd offered superior substitution, it was the common practice to superimpose upon the Gregorian melody, at intervals of the fifth and the octave, one or two additional voices. At the beginning and the end of each "bar" and from time to time elsewhere, the descant must omit the pitch in plain contrapuntal relation to the melody; but it was otherwise free to move about, and its rhythm had considerable flexibility; for, while the plainsong proceeded in notes all of the same value, its hovering accompaniment might substitute for each "whole" note its equivalence in "divisions" (eighths, sixteenths, and the like). The descant seems, in short, to have been a floridly ornamented obligato.[95]

Commonly, though not without exception, Crashaw's method of construction was to match a stanza of the original with a stanza, ordinarily more spacious and elaborate, of his own. He did not attempt to reproduce the style and temper of the subjacent "plainsong"; indeed, he would undoubtedly have found it easier completely to recast the matter of his text, though, with originals of such authority, the procedure might have seemed to him irreverent; his versions, unequal in worth, succeed best when he allowed himself most latitude.

Aquinas' sequence for the Feast of Corpus Christi, a hymn meticulous in its doctrinal formulation and somewhat bare of images, gave Crashaw particular difficulty. Two of the stanzas, turned into prose, read thus: "To Christians is given the dogma that the bread passes into flesh and the wine into blood; what you do not feel, what you do not see, beyond the usual course of things, a lively faith will confirm. Under different appearances—signs, however, and not substances—lie things extraordinary: flesh for food, blood for potion; yet Christ remains entire under each species." The substance of these stanzas scarcely invites decoration. Crashaw turns "dogma" into the "Heaven-instructed house of Faith," inserts a paradox into the first stanza and a sensual application into the second: the result is still pedestrian. A few touches like the remark, upon the breaking of the Eucharistic wafer, that there is never "less than whole Christ in every crumb" or that other unauthorized line wishing "harps of heaven to hands of man" betray the descantor; but the whole performance shows constraint. The "Adoro Te," taking more liberty, succeeds much better as a poem in its own right. St. Thomas wrote, for first stanza,

Adore te devote, latens Deitas,
Quae sub his figuris vere latitas.
Tibi se cor meum totum subjicit
Quis te contemplans totum deficit.[96]

Above the slow melody, Crashaw's eight-line descant
hovers in rapid "divisions":

With all the powers my poor Heart hath
Of humble love and loyall Faith,
Thus low (my hidden life!) I bow to Thee,
Whom *too much love hath bow'd more low for
me.*
Down, down, proud sense! Discourses dy
Keep close, my soul's inquiring ey!
Nor touch nor tast must look for more,
But each sitt still in his own Dore.[97]

The italicized figures have no warrant in the plainsong.

The "Dies Irae," sequence for requiem masses, and
by common consent the masterpiece of the medieval
hymns, is itself a *tuba, mirum spargens sonum,* impressive by virtue of its awful and solemn melody.
To harmonize it, to sweeten it by adding the soft
voices of viols and recorders, seems supererogation if
not profanation. Crashaw has written an affecting and
pathetic version, but one quite lacking the trumpet's
clangor. From striking conceits he desists, save for
that of the staggering stars; but he introduces some

rhetorical turns and some alliterations inappropriate to accompany so somber an original.

In his vernacular "laudi spirituali" a mystical poet, Jacopone da Todi, exhibited, in the "Stabat Mater," a tenderness and a passion congenial to Crashaw: imaginatively he became a participant in the scene on Calvary, stood, with the Blessed Virgin, "fount of love," beneath the cross, begged that the wounds of the crucified one might be implanted in his own heart; that he might share with Christ His pains and with the Blessed Mother her tears; that he might become intoxicated by the blood of Christ, enkindled and inflamed by love.

Da Todi's poem proposed motifs which obsessed Crashaw: the Mother of Sorrows, and the Crucified Christ; the tears, the blood, the Virgin's sword, and the Son's wounds; inflammation and inebriation; and it proposed them in a style which, if simpler than the baroque descant to be superimposed, is already rhetorically and musically rich. "Sancta Maria Dolorum," one of Crashaw's masterpieces, metaphorizes much which in the "Stabat Mater" is prose statement. What are isolated motifs in da Todi become recurrent and ritual in Crashaw; and the relations between Christ and His Mother form a perpetual and reciprocal movement. His nails write swords upon her heart; her swords of sympathetic pain turn into spears as He suffers in her suffering at His suffering. Her eyes bleed tears; His wounds weep blood. The "wing'd wounds" fly rapidly be-

tween them, till they mix wounds, and become one
crucifix. Then to this drama of the two who are one is
added a third, the compassionate poet who rebukes
himself for the inadequacy of his compassion; and
the intent is to draw the third, this "younger brother,"
more and more closely into the union. The stanzas
vary in metaphorical concentration, and the ode
should have ended (where Crashaw's fidelity to his
original did not permit) at the penultimate; stanzas
nine and ten introduce figures from accounting
(share, dividend, sum) which are incongruous with
the other motifs and with the liturgical fabric; but
the poem as a whole nowhere lapses much in temper-
ature—indeed, better perhaps, than any poem of
Crashaw's, moves climactically. This is the most successful of Crashaw's paraphrases, for, though he has
appropriated the substance of da Todi's poem, he has
completely reshaped it, translated it into his own
sensibility as well as into English, and made of his
version an independent work of art.

> O costly intercourse
> Of deaths, and worse,
> Divided loves. While son and mother
> Discourse alternate wounds to one another;
> Quick Deaths that grow
> And gather, as they come and goe:
> His Nailes write swords in her, which soon her
> heart
> Payes back with more then their own smart

Her *Swords*, still growing with his pain,
Turn *Speares*, and straight come home again.
. . . .
    O you, your own best Darts
    Dear, dolefull hearts!
    Hail; and strike home and make me see
That wounded bosomes their own weapons be.
    Come wounds! come darts!
    Nail'd hands! and peirced hearts!
Come your whole selves, sorrow's great son and
    mother!
    Nor grudge a yonger-Brother
Of greifes his portion, who (had all their due)
One single wound should not have left for you.

The style is superficially imagistic, with its spears
and swords and fires and floods. But the context
makes it clear that the reader is not intended to
visualize these objects. They are like the ideograms
of the Chinese alphabet—pictures which are shorthand for concepts; and this poetry is no longer really
Marinist. Crashaw started out with a devotion to
the literal wounds of Christ and the literal tears of
the Magdalen. In his later poetry, this kind of
physical devotion has disappeared, though all of its
imagery remains. Wounds become translatable as
mediatorial or mystical sufferings; tears are to be read
as penitential sorrow; the floods and the fires are the
forces of dissolving flux and animating love: imagery
turns into symbolism.

5. VERSIFICATION:
FROM THE COUPLET TO THE ODE

SOME poets, like George Herbert, constantly experiment with new stanzas; like John Cleveland, some show such ingenuity at rhyming that the juxtapositions offer the agreeable shock of wit. Not so Crashaw. In rhyme he preferred the familiar, and the familiar to him, repeating his *hearts* and *darts* like so many traditional and dear pieties. Apparently constricted by the planned economy of a stanzaic pattern, he found eventual ease in fluid couplets.

Oddly, for one of his best known poems, the "Wishes," he devises his own stanza. The tercet had been favorite with Ben Jonson, but Crashaw, taking it over, arranges its three verses in ascending lengths, from two feet to four. In one of the epigrams paraphrased from his own Latin, he employs an analogous tercet, diminishing his verses from six feet to four. The "Sospetto" follows the *ottava rima* of Marino's *La Strage*; "A Hymne of the Nativity" uses a six-line stanza; two poems on Christ's wounds use the alternately rhymed quatrain.

These instances are, however, exceptional, for habitually, Crashaw writes couplets. Even among his epigrams, the majority, though quatrains, are rhymed in pairs. Nor was this practice confined to any single period of his development: the early translations from Moschus, Catullus, Vergil, and Horace; the many poems in celebration of Their Majesties

and the royal offspring; "Music's Duel," and the
Teresa poems—all sustain it.

From the first, however, Crashaw was urged in
two directions. His taste for point and antithesis impelled him to the end-stopped distich, the English
counterpart of Ovid's elegiac verse.[98]

> Come death, come bands, nor do you shrink, my
>   eares,
> At those hard words mans cowardise calls feares.
> Save those of feare, no other bands feare I;
> Nor other death then this; the feare to die.[99]

But he was increasingly drawn to a rhetoric characterized not by tightness and economy but by relaxa-
tion and improvisatory exuberance.

In 1657, Cowley published his Pindaric Odes,
which set the fashion for a variety of poem much
practiced during the sequent century. Often bombas-
tic and grandiloquent, it deserved, by more than its
"irregular and lawless versification," the damnation
visited upon it by Dr. Johnson. From one point of
view, it was a timid approach to a freer kind of verse,
for the lines might vary in length, and without pattern or precedent, from two feet to six; from another,
it might be regarded as anticipating the imminent
reign of heroics, for it was prevalently rhymed, in
couplets. Donne and Jonson and their "sons" wrote
their lyrics in stanza forms, often elaborate; they
used the distich for their satires and didactic poems.
The Cowleyan ode, in the name of sublimity, curi-

ously mixes the "kinds." Whatever its intent, it made for the breakdown of poetic architecture and lent itself to the effect of improvisation.

Today Cowley has been acquitted of ignorance concerning the nature of Pindar's odes: he knew, as do we, that they were divided into strophe, antistrophe, and epode; knew, also, that their "numbers" were not really irregular. Consciously, he sought to produce an equivalence in English verse to the dithyrambic effect he felt in the Greek.

Cowley was not, however, the inventor of the irregular ode, but only its first systematic and avowed employer. The form—if it can be called that—has been traced back of Cowley to Drummond, Milton, Herbert, Carew, and Cartwright.[100] Then, too, Renaissance Latin poets, not content with reproducing the forms of Horace and Pindar, experimented with freer combinations. Scaliger gave the authority of his learning to such ventures, and himself used, in a single poem, thirty-three different meters. First publicly appearing in England by 1603, the "mixed ode" combined, in continuously printed lines, two or more classical stanza forms. The dithyramb, as it was sometimes called, pursued no stanzaic scheme; and, though all the individual lines can be scanned, uniformity of meter gives place to utmost diversity: though trochaic and iambic lines of varying lengths predominate, there are anapaestic and dactyllic substitutions.[101]

Herbert's "The Collar" is dithyrambic; the

"mixed ode" is represented by such poems as "Christ-mas," "Vanity," and "An Offering," which, having begun in one stanza pattern, terminate in another.

Crashaw did his distinctive work in these forms. Nor was this, as used to be supposed, the consequence of Cowley's influence. Obviously, any possible debt was Cowley's, for the Pindaric Odes were not com-posed till after 1651, when Crashaw had been two years dead.[102] Indeed, the freer forms first appeared in the 1646 edition of *Steps to the Temple*, though they were numerous and more developed in the edi-tion of 1648.

Among Crashaw's Latin poems are five dithy-rambs, four of which—"In Apollinem depereuntem Daphnen," "Aeneas Patris sui bajulus," "In Pigmali-ona," and "Arion"—are modeled on "Pasiphaes Fabula," a poem published in 1590 utilizing, in its twenty-two lines, each in a different meter, the full prosodic resources of Horace.[103]

For his experiments, therefore, Crashaw had the precedent of Renaissance Latin poetry. In his own English verse, however, he made more frequent and characteristic use of the liberty; and "free" verse becomes increasingly prominent as one follows the poet's chronological development. In translating his own Latin quatrains into English verse, he frequently substitutes another and more ample form; but of special and prophetic interest are the epigrams in which he experiments. The quatrain, "Ego sum ostium," becomes, in paraphrase,

And now th'art set wide ope, The Speare's sad Art,
Lo! hath unlockt thee at the very Heart:
    Hee to himselfe (I feare the worst)
        And his owne hope
    Hath *shut* these Doores of Heaven, that durst
        Thus set them *ope*.[104]

Having begun as a couplet with promise of a complementary twin, the epigram terminates with an alternately rhymed quatrain; the pentameter line has shrunk to a four alternating with a two.

The change in a poem of so brief compass seems, if its case be taken in isolation, an accident if not a mishap. Crashaw, one thinks, miscalculated and then forgot to revise his first draft, putting the whole into couplets or into a pair of quatrain stanzas. But the short set contains two analogous pieces.

In the same group, four epigrams illustrate another pattern: that of what may be called diminishing couplets, a pentameter line rhyming with one which is trimeter or dimeter.

Let it no longer be a forlorne hope
    To wash an Æthiope;
He's washt, His gloomy skin a peacefull shade
    For his white soule is made:
And now, I doubt not, the Eternall Dove,
    A black-fac'd house will love.[105]

In these two patterns are given the essentials of the seventeenth-century Pindarics: rhyming in couplets as the norm; double latitude of so joining verses uneven in length and of occasionally substituting the quatrain or some other vestigial stanza.

Crashaw's whole movement was toward the "form" thus prefigured; and in well-nigh all of his important mature poetry, and notably in the work which first appeared in the volumes of 1648 and 1652, he writes the irregular ode or dithyramb.

In the 1646 edition of *Steps to the Temple,* there appeared a set of verses, "On a prayer booke sent to Mrs. M. R." Though printed in stanzas, the poem follows no pattern; the strophes vary in length from four to fifteen lines; the verse lengths constantly shift; and, though the rhyming is predominantly by couplets, the alternately rhymed quatrain or other episodic variant may interpose.

> It is the Armory of light,
> Let constant use but keep it bright,
>   Youl find it yeelds
> To holy hands, and humble hearts,
>   More swords and sheilds
> Then sinne hath snares, or hell hath darts.
>
> Onely bee sure,
> The hands bee pure,
> That hold these weapons, and the eyes
> Those of turtles, chast, and true,
>   Wakefull, and wise
> Here is a friend shall fight for you,
> Hold but this booke before your heart,
> Let prayer alone to play his part. . . .

Reprinted, slightly enlarged, in 1648, it appeared, without strophic divisions, under the title, "An Ode Prefixed to a Prayer-booke. . . ." [106]

Though "Prayer" is Crashaw's single titular ode, it does not differ in character from the "Assumption," also published in 1646, and written in pentameter and tetrameter couplets interspersed with three groups of shorter verses rhymed *a a b c c b.*

The second (1648) edition of *Steps* included a group of irregular odes apparently composed since 1646.[107] As, with the exception of the address to the Countess of Denbigh, the *Carmen Deo Nostro* (1652) only reprints, sometimes in expanded or revised versions, the poems first appearing in 1648, these odes—among them, "The Flaming Heart," "Sancta Maria Dolorum," "A Hymne for the Epiphanie," and "On the Name of Jesus"—represent Crashaw's latest manner.

In some of them, the irregularities are slight. The elaborate ten-line stanzas of "Sancta Maria" end in tetrameter couplets for the first six stanzas; for the last five, in pentameter couplets. In "The Flaming Heart," a hundred and eight verses in length, and throughout rhymed in couplets, the tetrameter line predominates; but the poem opens with a pentameter couplet, uses the pentameter couplet from the seventy-seventh to the ninety-third line and elsewhere, and employs occasional couplets uniting a tetrameter and a pentameter.

"The Office of the Holy Crosse" abounds in ex-

periments. The Hymn for the Sixt opens with four
tetrameter couplets, follows with one in pentameter;
the concluding couplet ends with a heptameter line.
The Hymn for the Ninth Hour starts with a hexameter line and stops with a heptameter. The brilliant Hymn for Evensong, in the same office, varies,
in eight lines, between the tetrameter and the heptameter, and concludes:

> Gather now thy Greif's ripe *Fruit*. Great
>   mother-maid!
> Then sitt thee down, and sing thine Ev'n-
>   song in the sad *Tree's* shade.

Much the most elaborate of Crashaw's odes is the
symphonic "To the Name above Every Name." In
this rhapsody of two hundred and thirty-nine lines,
the tetrameter couplet is the norm again, and the
rhyming is predominantly in couplets; but the couplets range from dimeter to tetrameter, and the
intervals between the rhyming words are considerable. This ode is Crashaw's chief achievement in
the form toward which his talents inclined him.
Throughout, the variations in rhythm are subtle;
particularly sensitive is the sudden *largando* toward
the end of the poem when, after a perfumed passage,
the mood changes, the pace grows more solemn, the
tetrameter couplets lengthen into pentameter, the
short sentences give place to longer and more compli-
cated structures escaping conformity to the main pattern. Nor is the shift mere artifice: it corresponds to

a change in the theme. Crashaw has been considering, in sweet metaphors, the joys of mystical union; and, suddenly, with a sharp transition almost elliptical, he rebukes the softness of an age which seeks for a painless joy, for the martyrs' comfort without their agony.

How many Thousand Mercyes there
In Pitty's soft lap ly a sleeping!
Happy he who has the art
    To awake them,
    And to take them
*H*ome, and lodge them in *h*is *H*eart.
O that it *w*ere as it *w*as *w*ont to be!
*W*hen thy old *F*reinds of *F*ire, All *f*ull of Thee,
*F*ought against *F*rowns with smiles; gave
    *G*lorious chase
To Persecutions; And against the *F*ace
Of *D*eath and *f*eircest *D*angers, *d*urst with Brave
And sober pace *m*arch on to *m*eet a Grave.
On their *B*old *B*reasts about the world they *b*ore
    thee,
And to the *T*eeth of Hell *st*ood up to *t*each thee,
In *C*enter of their inmost *S*oules, they wore thee,
Where *R*ackes and *T*orments *st*riv'd, in vain,
    to *r*each thee . . .
Each wound of Theirs was Thy new Morning;
And *r*einthron'd thee in thy *R*osy Nest,
With *b*lush of thine own *B*lood thy day adorning,

It was the witt of love o'reflowd the Bounds
Of *W*rath, and made thee *w*ay through All Those
    *W*ounds.[108]

This passage exhibits Crashaw's phonetic prowess.
Alliteration, like every other kind of adornment and
enrichment, attracted him. In general, only significant words are so emphasized; but the sequences are
not conceived of in terms of line-units but rather as
ligatures between successive lines.

To talk of alliteration, or mastery of alliteration,
without reference to the effect it subserves would be
mechanical. The habitual, fond use of it, allies Crashaw to Poe, to Lanier, to Swinburne, to Francis
Thompson, to Father Hopkins—all poets with
whom, in other respects, he invites comparison. His

Making his mansion in the mild
And milky soul of a soft child

evokes anticipations of

The lilies and languors of virtue
For the raptures and roses of vice;

of Lanier's "Wisdoms ye winnow from winds that
pain me"; of Poe's "The viol, the violet, and the
vine"; of Hopkins'

In crisps of curl off wild winch whirl, and pour
And pelt music, till none's to spill nor spend.

In all these poets, poetry aspires to the condition
of music—that is, to "linked sweetness long drawn

out," effecting this by avoiding the explosive consonants save where they can be alliterated or otherwise
patterned, seeking to mollify the language with as
many "liquids" and semivowels as possible. Alliteration may, of course, be primarily structural, as in Old
English verse, where it marks the stresses, and occasionally in neoclassical verse, where it underlines an
antithesis; but, in modern times, it has chiefly served
as ornamentation, as harmonic enrichment; and while
it is likely, as in *Euphues,* to form patterns and to
connect groups of relatively important words, the
effect to the ear, when alliteration is a dominant feature of the style, is, undeniably, not to set off words
in bold relief but to blend and blur them in a mellif-
luous glide. If not checked by the jealous mind, the
ear becomes absorbed in listening to the sequences of
assonance and consonance; and the poem becomes a
composition in tones.

Poetry exists in a tension between music and philosophy: each critic has his own recipe for the proportion of the ingredients; Aristotle assimilates
poetry to philosophy; Poe, to music. The poets di-
verge as widely as the critics. Donne and Crashaw,
conventionally linked together, are remote if one
contrasts the cerebral propensity of the one with the
other's chant.

A fondness for alliteration—like a fondness for
feminine rhymes, for internal or frequently recurrent rhymes, for trisyllabic measures and for frequent
trisyllabic substitutions—is symptomatic of the poets

little given to dialectic. "Take care of the sound and
the sense will take care of itself" caricatures their
maxim; but, for their temptation, the sound of one
word will suggest its fellow, with consequent dangers
to concepts and architecture.

The severer classicists like Campion and Milton
would, indeed, regard rhyme itself as the original
sin; for rhyme, said Milton, is "the invention of a
barbarous age, to set off wretched matter . . . ; as
a thing of itself, to all judicious ears, trivial and of
no true musical delight: which consists only in apt
numbers, . . . not in the jingling sound of like endings, a fault avoided by the learned Ancients. . . ." [109]
But why, indeed, meter? Is not that, too, an ornament, not the essence, of poetry? The opposite of
poetry is not prose but science, say philosophical
critics; another group, "pure" intellectualists or
moralists, will judge meter a distraction: the business
of literature is to teach the truth; the movement of
meter so stirs the emotions as to impede attention to
the doctrine.

We might indeed schematize the poets according
to their use of sensuous media: those who habitually
write in blank verse; those who compose in rhyming
couplets or stanzas; those who added to end-rhyming
the extra resources of initial and internal rhyming—
for whom, that is, rhyme is a privilege and not a
duty: the progress will be in general from the most
meditative to the most musical poets, from those who
think in verse to those who sing.

Are meter and rhyme stimulants or narcotics?
According to Coleridge, "Metre in itself is simply a
stimulant of the attention . . ."; but "attention" is
ambiguous.[110] Perfect regularity of meter (the exactly periodic recurrence of strong stresses) produces
the nursery rhyme or the gospel hymn, concentrates
the emotions into a hypnoidal state; it lulls or opiates
the strictly intellectual faculties; it induces, on the
part of the reader, an emotional receptivity, weakens
his censorship of attitudes or sentiments expressed
by the poet. Intellectual attention is aroused not by
obedience to the meter but by deviations from it,
by tension between the pattern and its variants
or substitutions—heavy unstressed syllables, light
stresses, extra syllables, pauses, and rests. "The purpose of rhythm," says Yeats, "is to prolong the moment of contemplation, the moment when we are both
asleep and awake, . . . by hushing us with an allur-
ing monotony, while it holds us waking by variety. . . ."[111]

The effect of rhyme is always sensuous, never
intellectual; but its more specific effect depends upon
its position and its degree of freshness. If, as in
Browning's "Last Duchess," the rhyme rarely coin-
cides with a strong stress or a full stop, the ordinary
ear takes the verse as "blank"; in general, rhyme is
less heard in enjambed than in closed couplets. If,
again, the stanza form is elaborate and the recurrences
of a rhyme are distant from one another, the ear,
unless warned and abnormally attentive, is likely to

miss the prepared concord. Many poets have valued
triumph over self-imposed handicaps and have exe-
cuted rhymed patterns of which only the eye—and
especially the eye of the fellow craftsman—takes
note. The effect of this subtlety, which reduces rhyme
to assonance, is to minimize the irrational pleasure in
sound which emerges most obviously in couplets or
other close juxtapositions of the rhyme.

The novelty or familiarity of the *similiter desi-
nentia* alters the hearer's response. Highly ingenious
rhyming—like that of Frere, of Browning, of Byron,
of W. S. Gilbert—attracts specific attention to itself
and seems appropriate only to satire or fantasy. Trite-
ness of rhyme, or the constant recurrence of the same,
would, like regularity of meter, produce a hypnoidal
state.

Campion, attacking rhyme as a mere *figura verbi*,
links it with "following of the letter," or alliteration;
and, for the austere rationalist, both are alike offen-
sive as pleasures purely sensuous. Yet does the case
for meter repose upon a foundation more secure? It,
too, offers pleasure to the senses. Renaissance moralists, conscious that poetry owed its dignity and intellectual status to the "ideas" conveyed through it, had
always to defend the sensuous pleasure of verse on
the plea that, mnemonic device, it enabled men to
store their memories with *loci communes* or that, like
the syrup which sweetens the medicinal cup, it in-
duced children of all ages to imbibe instruction.[112] The
moralist might therefore content himself with passing

judgment upon the "ideas" promulgated through verse; if they are "sound," then the more seductive the inducements the more widely disseminated will be the ideas.

As Crashaw was drawn to opposite genres, the epigram and the ode, so rival impulses appear in his latest poetry. His "conceits" and paradoxes, figures appropriate to a religion of marvel, were intended to amaze; but his music of rhyme, assonance, and consonance aims at a hypnoidal or ecstatic state.[113] This antithesis is probably, however, too strong. Many of his paradoxes, oxymora, and *concetti* were at once so familiar in the Italian literature upon which he founded his taste and so reiterated in his own poetry that, for him, at least, their shock must have been diminished to a shorthand formula for miracle. Indeed for one who, after some familiarity with Marinism and Jesuit literature, reads Crashaw, the repetition of rhymes and images will make the poet's own aim seem rather hypnotic and ruminative than arresting.

The "Song" which follows the Teresan cycle seems, in its manipulation of end-stopped couplets, oxymoron, antimetabole, and alliteration, to be definitely incantatory.[114]

> Lord, when the sense of thy sweet grace
> Sends up my soul to seek thy face.
> Thy blessed eyes breed such desire
> I dy in love's delicious Fire.
>   O love, I am thy *Sacrifice*.

Be still triumphant, blessed eyes.
Still shine on me, fair suns! that I
Still may behold, though still I dy.
   Though still I dy, I live again;
Still longing so to be still slain,
So gainfull is such losse of breath,
I dy even in desire of death.
   Still live in me this loving strife
Of living *Death* and dying *Life*.
For while thou sweetly slayest me
Dead to my selfe, I live in Thee.

For any habitual reader of Crashaw, this poem offers no novelties of figure and it is devoid of images; it is an epitome of stock figures and phrases, a ritual assembled for the purpose of putting poet—and reader—into a trance state. From its position after the three meditations on the figure of St. Teresa, it is to be assumed that it represents an application to the emotions of what had previously been proposed to the imagination; it is an affective refrain to the whole trio.

In substance, but few of Crashaw's poems are "mystical." If, in spite of that, the name has affixed itself to them and is felt to have at least vague relevance, it is that their aim, especially in the odes, seems the production of ecstásy, a poetic equivalent to the trance state of the mystics. We are invited to concentrate our attention upon some sensuous object like the crucifix, some sensuous symbol like wounds or tears, while the poet, by means of meter, liturgical rhymes, assonance, and alliteration, creates an atmosphere which lulls the critical intellect while the poem insistently repeats its motif.

How does hypnotic poetry differ from "bad" verse? In the degree of control exercised by the poet. Bad poetry chiefly celebrates themes so commonly accepted as "idealistic"—for the nineteenth century, themes like home, mother, childhood, love of nature, and patriotism—that the poet has but to propose the theme in some familiar and regular meter; after a line or two, the reader, lulled by the rhythm, escapes into composing an idyll of his own.[115] Bad poetry induces auto-hypnosis. Good poetry, of whatever sort, never ceases to control and manipulate the reader's sensibility: the images and words must be sharp enough, the poet's mind sufficiently sure, vigorous, and subtle, so that the reader is drawn out of himself. If it be hypnotic poetry, the thoughts operative must be those of the operator, not of the patient.

The hypnotic intent of Crashaw's poetry has been little observed because most English readers have, in preoccupation and attitude, been too alien to him for the establishment of initial confidence. For such effect as his odes design, the reader—through kinship in sensibility or through religious orientation or both —must be susceptible to such control.

6. SYMBOLISM

THE POET's birthright, his imagery, is that part of
him which is least controllable by effort and discipline. His sensuous aridity or fertility; the relative
predominance of eye over ear or of both over the
nostrils; his sensitivity to tint and shade or his bold
reduction to line drawing or charcoal sketch; the
precision of his observation or his subjective diminu-
tions and hyperboles; the domains from which he
elicits his tropes—whether moor and mountain, or
cathedral and drawing room, from natural history or
unnatural: these aesthetic characters reveal his breed.
Doubtless the poet as self-critic can prune the luxuriance of the imagery, make austere sacrifice of those
clusters growing in contiguity too close; but the kind
of grapes he rears owes dependence to soil and cli-
mate. So far, that is, as imagery is not pastiche and
imitation, it lays bare the temperamental self and can
change its character only as, and so far as, the poet is
susceptible of personal conversion.

In his life alone does Nature live. Even among
the romantic poets, one notes their unconscious selection from what they have experienced. The spirit of
Childe Harold finds representative embodiment in
the vast and horrendous, in altitude and solitude—
the ocean, the mountain, the storm; Shelley, the
aerial, in the cloud, the skylark, the west wind;
Wordsworth in the quietly pastoral, the landscape

domesticated by man or indwelt and tempered by the World Spirit.

All imagery is double in its reference, a composite of perception and conception. Of these ingredients, the proportions vary. The metaphorist can collate image with image, or image with concept, or concept with image, or concept with concept. He can compare love to a rose, or a rose to love, or a pine grove to a cathedral, or religious ecstasy to intoxication. Then, too, the metaphorists differ widely in the degree of visualization for which they project their images. The epic simile of Homer and of Spenser is fully pictorial; the intent, relative to the poet's architecture, is decorative. On the other hand, the "sunken" and the "radical" types of imagery [116]—the conceits of Donne and the "symbols" of Hart Crane—expect scant realization by the senses.

Symbolism may be defined as imagery understood to imply a conceptual meaning: such definition is latitudinarian enough to admit the poetry of Mallarmé as well as the ceremonial of the Church. The concept may be a mere overtone, a darkly descried vista, or it may be a category susceptible of prose statement. Some symbolisms are private, founded upon the poet's childhood associations of thing and sentiment; without biographical aid, the reader is likely to find them mere imagism or a congeries of oddly juxtaposed perceptions. Others—like the Christian emblems of dove, lamb, shepherd, cross—

are communal. Others must be well-nigh universal, even to men topographically untraveled: the plain, the mountain, the valley, the ocean, the storm, darkness and light, are broadly human.

Parable and allegory may be defined as symbolic narratives in which a conceptual sequence runs parallel to—or, rather, is incarnate in—an imaginative sequence; they are, too, the most explicit forms. Christ parabolically identifies himself with the Good Shepherd; the Word, with the seed; the fig tree, with the unproductive life. Spenser and Bunyan label their persons and places: the Giant Despair, Fidessa, Orgolio, Mr. Worldly Wiseman, Faithful; the Bower of Bliss, the House of Holiness, Doubting Castle, the Delectable Mountains.

The proportion of strength between the image and the concept ranges widely. In eighteenth-century personification, the picture frequently evaporated till but a capital remained; in Mallarmé, the imagery only is presented, though, by its lack of naturalistic congruence, its disjunction, it disturbs the consciousness till the latter evokes some coherent psychological pattern for which all the images are relevant.

Crashaw, sensuous of temperament, wrote a poetry mellifluously musical, lavishly imagistic. At first acquaintance it seems the song of the nightingale hovering over her skill, "bathing in streams of liquid melody"; later, it seems the passage work, the cadenzas, the glissandi of an endowed and muchschooled virtuoso. Yet his life shows him to have

been an ascetic, denying his senses all save their
homage to God. In turning to religion and religious
poetry, he "changed his object not his passion," as
St. Augustine said of the Magdalen: [117] the images
of his secular poetry recur in his sacred. He loves his
God as he might have loved his "supposed mistress."

Not a preacher or prophet, Crashaw had no
"message" to announce. He had suffered and exulted, and exulted in suffering; but his experiences
did not tempt him to philosophy or other prose
formulation. His was to be a poetry in which the
rhythms and images would tell their own tale.

To his symbolism he supplied no chart of prose
equivalents. Yet no reader has long studied his poems
without feeling that their imagery is more than
pageant; that, rather, it is a vocabulary of recurrent
motifs. [118]

Nor is this symbolism really undecipherable. In
the main it follows traditional Christian lines, drawing on the Bible, ecclesiastical lore, and the books of
such mystics as St. Bernard and St. Teresa. Even
when it is "private"—as, in some measure, every
poet's will be, it yields to persistent and correlating
study. Not widely ranging, Crashaw's images reappear in similar contexts, one event elucidating another. No casual reader of his poems, for example,
but has been arrested by the recurrence of "nest,"
usually in rhyming union with "breast"; and, surely,
no constant reader has long doubted its psychological
import, its equivalence to shelter, refuge, succor.

It need not be maintained—it is, indeed, incredible
—that Crashaw constructed a systematic symbolism.
It is unlikely, even, that he knew why certain images
possessed, for him, particular potence. Obviously
much concerned with his technique, given to revision,
a lover of the arts, he seems, as a man, ingenuous,
free from self-consciousness, imaginatively uncen-
sored.

In his steady movement from secular poetry to an
exclusive preoccupation with sacred, from Latin to
the vernacular, he relinquished—deliberately, it
would seem—the Renaissance decoration of classical
mythology. As a schoolboy he had written hymns to
Venus, poems on Pygmalion, Arion, Apollo and
Daphne, Aeneas and Anchises; and in his Latin
epigrams, and in "Music's Duel," there occur classical embellishments. From the English sacred poems,
however, such apparatus is conspicuously absent.
Giles Fletcher, of his English predecessors closest
to him in temper and idiom, had compared the
ascending Christ to Ganymede, snatched up from
earth to attend upon Jupiter; but no such bold cor-
relation of pagan and Christian finds place in Crashaw's poetry. Donne and Herbert, also erudites, had
made a similar surrender of their classicism; [119] and
to Herbert's example in particular he may have been
indebted.

Otherwise, Crashaw makes no attempt to differentiate his sacred from his secular imagery; many
characteristic figures and metaphors, "delights of the

Muses," are reënlisted in the service of Urania. For
example, the familiar paradox of the Incarnation,
whereby Jesus is at once the son and the father of
the Blessed Virgin, is anticipated in the apostrophe
to Aeneas carrying Anchises: "Felix! *parentis* qui
pater diceris esse tui!" [120] The persistent motif of
the mystical poems first appears in "Wishes":

> A well tam'd heart
> For whose more noble smart
> Love may bee long chusing a Dart.

Unlike Herbert, Crashaw rarely recollects homely
images of market place and fireside; and allusions to
the polities and economies of the Stuart world come
but seldom. Christ, dying, is called "his own legacy."
With the Blessed Virgin, Crashaw, who, too, has set
"so deep a share" in Christ's wounds, would draw
some "dividend." To these financial metaphors, one
may add what at first view seems Herbertian—the
angels with their bottles, and the breakfast of the
brisk cherub.[121] Yet, though "breakfast" Herbert
would surely not have disdained, such intimacy with
the habits of cherubs is peculiarly alien to the Anglican spirit of *The Temple*. It is Mary's tears which,
having wept upwards, become, at the top of the
milky river, the cream upon which the infant angel
is fed, adding "sweetnesse to his sweetest lips"; and
this context, by its extravagant lusciousness, reduces
the blunt word to but a passing grotesquerie.

Some feeling for Nature, especially the dawn and

flowers, the young Crashaw undoubtedly had; but even the early poems evince no botanical niceness, no precision of scrutiny. The first of the Herrys poems develops a single metaphor, that of a tree whose blossoms, ravished by a mad wind, never deliver their promised fruit; but unlike Herbert's "orange tree," this is a tree of no specific genus.[122] Crashaw's habitual blossoms are the conventional lily and rose.

These flowers, which appear briefly, in his earliest poems, as outward and visible creatures, do not disappear from his later verse; but they soon turn into a ceremonial and symbolical pair, a liturgical formula, expressive of white and red, tears and blood, purity and love. Already in the panegyric on the Duke of York, lines which begin with a delicate naturalism end, with a reduction to liturgical red and white, in a prefigurement of Crashaw's final style.

So have I seene (to dresse their Mistresse *May*)
Two silken sister flowers consult, and lay
Their bashfull cheekes together, newly they
Peep't from their buds, shew'd like the Gardens
    eyes
Scarce wakt: like was the Crimson of their joyes,
Like were the Pearles they wept. . . .[123]

In the "Bulla," or "Bubble," the flowers have become antithetic colors in shifting transmutations.[124] If Crashaw's *flora* soon turn symbols, his *fauna* have never owed genuine allegiance to the world of

Nature. The worm; the wolf, the lamb; the fly, the
bee; the dove, the eagle, the "self-wounding pelican," and the phoenix: all derive their traits and their
significance from bestiary or Christian tradition, not
from observation; and their symbolism is palpable.
In their baseness men are "all-idolizing worms"; in
their earthly transience and fickleness and vanity,
foolish wanton flies. The bee, a paragon of industry,
is still more a creator, preserver, or purveyor of
mystic sweetness. The Holy Name of Jesus is adored
by angels that throng

> Like diligent Bees, And swarm about it.
>   O they are wise;
> And know what *Sweetes* are suck't from out it.
>   It is the Hive,
>   By which they thrive,
> Where all their Hoard of Hony lyes.

The dove and lamb, of frequent appearance, be-
token innocence and purity; they are also meet for
votive offering. Sometimes the doves emblemize elect
souls, whose eyes should be "Those of turtles, chaste,
and true"; sometimes, the Holy Ghost. The *Agnus
Dei*, the white lamb slain before the foundation of
the world, was Crashaw's favorite symbol for Christ
and for him, among all symbols, one of the most
affecting.

"By all the Eagle in thee, all the dove": so
Crashaw invokes the chaste Teresa, the mystic whose

wings carried her high, whose spiritual vision was unflinching and acute.

> Sharpe-sighted as the Eagles eye, that can
> Out-stare the broad-beam'd Dayes Meridian.

Meditating her books, the responsive reader finds his heart "hatcht" into a nest "Of little Eagles, and young loves." [125]

To the phoenix, Crashaw devoted a Latin poem, a "Genethliacon et Epicedion," in which the paradox of a fecund death shows its expected fascination for him. The fragrant, unique, and deathless bird re-appears in the Latin epigrams, and in the English poems, both secular and sacred. It occurs twice in the sequence of Herrys elegies; it is belabored at length in the panegyric to Henrietta Maria, "Upon her Numerous Progenie," where it becomes a symbol of supreme worth. In the sacred poems, it assumes its traditional Christian office as sign of the God-man, virgin-born, only-begotten, and immortal.

With most artists, the pleasures of sight are pre-eminent; with Crashaw, in spite of his interest in pictures and emblems, the fuller-bodied and less sharply defined senses would appear to have afforded richer, more characteristic delight.

His colors are elementary, chiefly conventional, readily symbolic. In his religious poetry, but three oc-cur: red (or purple = *purpureus*), with its traditional relation, through fire and the "Flaming Heart" to love; black; and white. Black is, for him, the sign not of mourning or penitence but of sin and, still more, of finiteness, of mortality: "Dust thou art, and to dust thou shalt return." In his translation of Catullus, men are "dark Sons of Sorrow." Augmented, the phrase reappears in "The Name of Jesus" as "dark Sons of Dust and Sorrow." Elsewhere in the religious poems, man is "Disdainful dust and ashes" or "Darke, dusty Man."

White, perhaps as the synthesis of all colors, perhaps as the symbol of luminous purity, is the most exalting adjective in Crashaw's vocabulary. It occurs in his secular verse, especially in his panegyrics upon the royal family. But it is more frequent in his *carmina sacra*, used customarily of the Blessed Virgin or Christ, and most strikingly of Christ as the Lamb.

> Vain loves, avaunt! bold hands forbear!
> The Lamb hath dipp't his white foot here.[126]

The absence from the religious poetry of green, the color of nature, and blue—in the tradition of Christian art, the color of truth and of the Blessed Virgin —is conspicuous; so is the absence of chiaroscuro. By other means, he produces a sensuous luxuriance; but, in respect to the palette, he turns, like the Gospels, to bold antithesis of black and white.

For evidence that Crashaw was a lover of music, one need not appeal to "Music's Duel." "On the Name of Jesus," among his four or five masterpieces, calls to celebration all sweet sounds of instrument—

> Be they such
> As sigh with supple wind
> Or answer Artfull Touch. . . .

These flutes, lutes, and harps are the "Soul's most certain wings," Heaven on Earth; indeed, in a moment of quasi-Platonic identification of reality with highest value he equates "All things that Are" with all that are musical. Assuredly, Crashaw intended his own poetry to be—what by virtue of his mastery of vowel and consonant sequences and alliteration it habitually is—sweet to the ear, Lydian. But, for him, it is also true, human music was an initiation into an archetypal music, the harmonious concert of the spheres "which dull mortality more feels than hears." The ears are "tumultous shops of noise" compared with those inner sensibilities which, properly disciplined, may hear, as from afar, the inexpressive nuptial hymn.[127]

Crashaw's favorite adjectives, "sweet" and "delicious," mingle fragrance and taste. His holy odors are chiefly traditional—those of flowers and of spices. "Let my prayer be set forth in Thy sight as the incense," said the Psalmist; but the simile finds its analogy in the ascent of both. The fragrance of spices pervades that manual of the mystics, the *Song of Songs*. To the Infant Jesus, the magi brought frankincense and myrrh. The Magdalen dies as "perfumes expire." The Holy Name is invoked as a "cloud of condensed sweets," bidden to break upon

us in balmy and "sense-filling" showers. In his ode
on Prayer, the most mystical of his poems, Crashaw
bids the lover of God, the virgin soul, to seize the
Bridegroom

> All fresh and fragrant as he rises
> Dropping with a baulmy Showr
> A delicious dew of spices. . . .

Sometimes Crashaw's gustatory delights, like those
of the

> sweet-lipp'd Angell-Imps, that swill their throats
> In creame of Morning *Helicon* . . .[128]

remain innocently physical. But customarily the
pleasure of the palate, too, becomes symbolic, as it is
when the Psalmist bids us "taste . . . how good the
Lord is." The angels who swarm about the Holy
Name are wise because they "know what Sweetes are
suck't from out of it." This palatal imagery might
be expected to culminate in apostrophes to the Blessed
Sacrament; but not so. For Protestants, the Holy
Communion is a symbolic as well as commemorative
eating and drinking; to Crashaw, who believed in
Transubstantiation, the miraculous feast seemed
rather the denial of the senses than their symbolic
employment. His expansive paraphrases of St.
Thomas' Eucharistic hymns are notably sparse in
sensuous imagery. It is not the Blood of Christ on
the altar but the redeeming blood on the cross which
prompts him to spiritual inebriation.

Crashaw's liquids are water (tears, penitence); milk (maternal succor, nutrition); blood (martyrdom on the part of the shedder, transference of vitality to the recipient); wine (religious inebriation, ecstasy). Fluid, they are constantly mixing in ways paradoxical or miraculous. In one of his earliest poems, a metrical version of Psalm 137, blood turns into water. In one of the latest, "Sancta Maria," "Her eyes bleed Teares, his wounds weep Blood." From the side of Christ, crucified, flowed an "amorous flood of Water wedding Blood." The angels, preparing for a feast, come with crystal phials to draw from the eyes of the Magdalen "their master's Water: their own Wine." Milk and blood may mingle, as when maternal love induces self-sacrifice; water turns to wine when tears of penitence become the happy token of acceptance and union; wine is transubstantiated into blood in the Sacrament; blood becomes wine when, "drunk of the dear wounds," the apprehender of Christ's redeeming sacrifice loses control of his faculties in an intoxication of gratitude and love.

The last of the senses is at once the most sensuous and the least localized. To it belong the thermal sensations of heat and chill. Fire, the cause of heat, is, by traditional use, the symbol of love; its opposites are ordinarily lovelessness and—what is the same— death. The "flaming Heart" of Christ or of the Blessed Virgin is the heart afire with love. St. Teresa's ardor renders her insensitive to love's antonym and opposite, the chill of the grave. Crashaw is likely to unite the opposites. Since she is both Virgin and Mother, Mary's kisses may either heat or cool. Lying between her chaste breasts, the Infant Jesus sleeps in snow, yet warmly.[129]

The supremities of touch, for Crashaw's imagination, are experienced in the mystical "wound of love," in martyrdom, and in nuptial union. In the former states, torment and pleasure mix: the pains are delicious; the joys, intolerable. In his mystical poems, Crashaw makes free use of figures drawn from courtship and marriage. Christ is the "Noble Bridegroom, the Spouse of Virgins." Worthy souls are those who bestow upon His hand their "heaped up, consecrated Kisses," who store up for Him their "wise embraces." The soul has its flirtations, its "amorous languishments," its "dear and divine annihilations." St. Teresa, love's victim, is sealed as Christ's bride by the "full Kingdom of that final Kiss"; and her mystic marriage has made her the mother of many disciples, many "virgin-births."

In the spirit of St. Ignatius' *Exercitia Spiritualia,* Crashaw performs an "Application of the Senses" upon all the sacred themes of his meditation. God transcends our images as He transcends our reason; but, argues the Counter-Reformation, transcension does not imply abrogation. Puritanism opposes the senses and the imagination to truth and holiness; for Catholicism, the former may be ministering angels. "How daring it is to picture the incorporeal," wrote

Nilus Scholasticus in the *Greek Anthology;* "but yet
the image leads us up to spiritual recollection of
celestial beings." [130] Not *iconoclasts,* some censors
would grant that visual imagery, emanating from
the "highest" of the senses, may point from the seen
to the unseen; there they would halt. Crashaw, like
one persistent school of mystics, would boldly appropriate the whole range of sensuous experience as
symbolic of the inner life.

Studied case by case, Crashaw's striking imagery
will yield its symbolic intent. But its most characteristic feature emerges only when image is collated
with image. Poetic symbolism may constantly devise
new alliances of sense and concept; indeed, the poet
Emerson objected to Swedenborg's "Correspondences" on the precise ground of their fixed and
systematic character. With Crashaw, though rigidity
is never reached, his metaphors yet form a series of
loosely defined analogies and antitheses and cross
references, a system of motifs symbolically expressive of themes and emotions persistently his.

Associated images recur like ceremonial formulas.
In the secular poems, the lily and the rose have
appeared, singly and together. The association continues into the religious poems, but the metaphorical
character of the flowers has become explicit. In the
epigram on the Holy Innocents, the mother's milk
and the children's blood turn, for Crashaw's pious
fancy, into lilies and roses. A characteristic later
juxtaposition, in the "Hymn for the Circumcision,"

gives the metamorphosis: "this modest Maiden Lilly,
our sinnes have sham'd into a Rose."

A similar ritual coupling is that of the pearl and
the ruby. Sometimes these symbols appear singly,
sometimes together. In the same "Hymn for the
Circumcision" Crashaw sees Christ's drops of blood
as rubies. The tears of the Magdalen are Sorrow's
"richest Pearles." They are united in the eighteenth
stanza of "Wishes." Still united, they reappear in
the religious poetry: When men weep over the
bloody wounds of Christ,

> The debt is paid in *Ruby*-teares,
> Which thou in Pearles did'st lend.[131]

Another frequent union—and this not of contrasts
but of contradictories—couples fire and water, an
oxymoron of images. Already, in an early poem, the
sun is represented as paying back to the sea in tears
what, as fire, it borrowed. When the Magdalen
washes Christ's feet with tears, wiping them with
her hair,

> Her eyes flood lickes his feets faire staine,
> Her haires flame lickes up that againe.
> This flame thus quench't hath brighter beames:
> This flood thus stained fairer streames.[132]

The Blessed Virgin is the "noblest nest Both of love's
fires and floods." The tears of contrition or of sorrow,
so far from extinguishing the fire of love, make it
burn more ardently.

But one cannot thus far have surveyed Crashaw's imagery without perceiving how the whole forms a vaguely defined but persistently felt series of inter-relations. There are things red—fire, blood, rubies, roses, wine—and things white—tears, lilies, pearls, diamonds: symbols of love and passion; symbols of contrition, purity, innocence.

On its sensuous surface, his imagination sparkles with constant metamorphosis: tears turn into soft and fluid things like milk, cream, wine, dew; into hard things like stars, pearls, and diamonds. Beneath, the same experiences engage poet and poem.

All things flow. Crashaw's imagery runs in streams; the streams run together; image turns into image. His metaphors are sometimes so rapidly juxtaposed as to mix—they occur, that is, in a suc-cession so swift as to prevent the reader from focus-ing separately upon each. The effect is often that of phantasmagoria. For Crashaw, the world of the senses was evidently enticing; yet it was a world of appearances only—shifting, restless appearances. By temperament and conviction, he was a believer in the miraculous; and his aesthetic method may be in-terpreted as a genuine equivalent of his belief, as its translation into a rhetoric of metamorphosis. If, in the Gospels, water changes to wine and wine to blood, Crashaw was but imaginatively extending this prin-ciple when he turned tears into pearls, pearls into lilies, lilies into pure Innocents.

Style must incarnate spirit. Oxymoron, paradox,

and hyperbole are figures necessary to the articulation of the Catholic faith. Crashaw's *concetti*, by their infidelity to nature, claim allegiance to the supernatural; his baroque imagery, engaging the senses, intimates a world which transcends them.

CHAPTER FIVE

THE REPUTATION

T HIS STUDY has been chiefly concerned with the meaning of Crashaw's poetry as it can be made out from a study of his context of time and place, associates, instruments of piety and sensibility, and predecessors in kind. The assumption of such study is that the meaning of poetry is primarily the poet's—his to endow, ours to inherit. But the meaning of artifacts is cumulative. Whenever a really original work of art is really apprehended, the accession alters the status and meaning of the existing "accredited" works. Thus, if Francis Thompson or Gerard Hopkins has excelled Crashaw at what he purposed or effected, we can dispense with Crashaw or lower him to the status of substitute, to be accepted only if the "original" is not on the shelves. His "meaning" to English poetry alters with the addition of cognate successors.[1] But his "meaning" changes also by virtue of subsequent patterns of thought.

To trace a poet's reputation is to trace the imposition upon him of patterns with which he was unfamiliar, meanings to which he would not have subscribed; but a poet's reputation, his record of scars and badges, is a part of his total meaning, not merely for cultural history but, at last, for his modern reader. It is indeed his seeming relevance to the present which motivates the re-creative study of his primary meaning.

The history of Crashaw's reputation brings into relief those features of his spirit and his style which have differentiated him from other poets.

To his work the eighteenth century paid some heed because he was the friend of Cowley and (as it was mistakenly believed) of Selden; because Mr. Pope had, in an early letter, written a critique of his poetry and, further, had condescended to borrow from it; because the elegant Mr. Hayley had praised him. Chiefly because Milton was supposed debtor to it, the "Sospetto" was acclaimed. But the Augustan ear was attuned to couplets more habitually "closed" than Crashaw's; and Pope felt superiorly incompetent to discuss Crashaw's "numbers": "they are so various and irregular, and mostly Pindaric." To Augustan rationalism, the extravagance and unnatural ingenuity of the conceit gave offense; Protestant taste was repelled by many of Crashaw's themes and by the baroque treatment of sanctities so solemn.

In the Romantic period, seventeenth-century prose and verse drama found fervent admirers; but, except with Coleridge and the American Transcendentalists, Crashaw and Donne did not. Though the Romantic critics had revolted against neoclassical didacticism, they sought to substitute the "natural," the spontaneous, the sentimental; according to their canons, the "Metaphysicals" were too cerebral or too labored to be truly poetic. Later in the nineteenth century, students, looking back, thought they discovered, in the sensuousness of Keats, in the fire of Shelley, analogues to those qualities of Crashaw which they could acclaim; still later, Swinburne and Francis Thompson, the most tropical of contemporary poets, were similarly, and with more justice, to recall their precursor. Throughout the century, however, there persisted as deterrents to Crashaw's reputation his conceits, his Tridentine Catholicism, and their union. For some critics, his conceits proved frigid: Francis Thompson, who might have been expected to synchronize with his predecessor's sensibility, thinks even "Music's Duel" is "too researched." Others denied the ice of the conceits but adjudged their very fire inappropriate to sacred poetry. Indeed, with a few exceptions, nineteenth-century Catholics were as distant from Crashaw's aesthetic as were Protestants and agnostics.[2]

Our own time is more generous. With the work of Wölfflin and Geoffrey Scott, the baroque has ceased to be synonymous with "decadent"; in the criticism of Grierson and Eliot, conceits, whether "metaphysical" or Marinist, are no longer dismissed as generically contemptible.

The causes for this change in attitude are various. For one, ours is an age so conscious of dead and of mutually contradictory dogmatisms as to be chary of

all absolutes, whether of faith or of taste. From the
nineteenth century onwards, the rapid development
of historical scholarship has made the literate aware
of cultural cycles and of the aesthetic pendulum;
and the consequence has been to make most of them
determinists in theory and, in practice, sceptical of
standards. Of course, few men succeed in consistency
of scepticism: if nothing else, their biological impera-
tives furnish attitudes to be rationalized; but a really
thoroughgoing scepticism could take no exception to
any pattern of life or of art, all illegitimacies being
"natural" and equal.

Another cause is the very oscillation of the pendulum which, making scholars into sceptics, has produced a current generation of poets, and readers of
poetry, ignorant of Browning and Tennyson but ad-
miring Donne, Pope, Emily Dickinson, and Father
Hopkins. Practicing poets can never, perhaps, really
relinquish thinking in terms of "kinds" and absolutes. Impossible for them is the scholarly dilet-
tante's relish of Chaucer, Racine, Cleveland, Wordsworth, and Whitman. Indeed, for distinguished
achievement in any of the arts, it appears indis-
pensable that the artist should believe implicitly that
there exists but one true method—his own; that
what he has to say, sing, or see is unique in its rightness.

"If Pope be not a poet, where is poetry to be
found?" asked Dr. Johnson, indignant at the War-
tons' suspicions. The question befitted the author of

London and *The Vanity of Human Wishes.* Poets must first of all believe in their own uniqueness and rightness; then next, they must believe that the real worth of their predecessors and their contemporaries depends upon the degree of kinship which they sustain to the true and real poetry, just as creative philosophers—Aristotle, Leibniz, Hegel, and Whitehead—have inevitably regarded their predecessors as groping toward the system now, at last, made manifest.

The rise in our day of poets who believe themselves the blood relatives of the complex and metaphorical poets of the seventeenth century has caused the modes of Donne, the Herberts, and Crashaw to seem, once again, living options and "true" as distinct from "quaint" poetry; and through the children we may come to a sympathetic concern with their ancestral pieties.

Both the erudite scepticism of critical absolutes and the faith in a particular poetic absolute shared by some contemporary poets have concurred in easing our access to Crashaw; furthermore, the obstacle of his religion has, in England and America, considerably diminished. The continuance of the Oxford Movement within the Anglican Church and the development of an intelligentsia within the Catholic have made the old Faith almost fashionable; Protestantism, grown liberal, can no longer dispense the old-fashioned acerbities; as for the younger "naturalist," he is not propitiated by "reduced" theologies and, like Santayana, respects most those forms of belief which are traditional, liturgical, and un-compromising.

Today, "imperfect sympathies" for Crashaw find their impediment in two suspicions, more often articulated in conversation than in public print, and more often felt than defined or avowed: his rhetoric and his temperament.

With most modernists, and with many belated romantics, rhetoric—word and thing—has fallen into disrepute as, like "ritual," incompatible with sincerity. Rhetoric has been disposed of as "mere," oratory as "empty"—as though it were impossible to say brilliantly what one utterly believes. In consequence, formal instruction in schemes and tropes has yielded place to exhortations inciting the self-expression of unformed selves. This dismissal of rhetoric rests upon two assumptions: that rhetorical training will impose, upon individual minds, a common and traditional discipline; and that a man really in earnest about his "ideas" cannot be bothered to express them exactly and compellingly. The first assumption is probably correct; and the question then remains whether we are to reject all studies which temper idiosyncrasy or impart our humane heritage. The second assumption is, at most, but half a truth. If a man who believes in his "ideas"—or in his emotions, for that matter—desires to communicate them persuasively to others, faith in his cause will give importance and "sincerity" to the means.

It is further to be considered that rhetoric like other skills—physical, social, and artistic—does not require from the practitioner the same self-conscious concentration which the auditor or spectator, himself an amateur, empathetically supplies. Bach and Milton, academically honored, are misread save by the mature. In both, the technical equipment—the control of fugal development or metrical, the capacity for long phrases and architectural planning—is likely to tax the auditor's attention, till the masters seem cerebral manipulators. Yet with both, learning and technique have become vehicular.

The whole problem of sincerity is difficult; and particular judgments of character are precarious. The charge of affectation often means little more than "Why do you pretend to be unlike me? Your complexities and subtleties are calculated exhibitions; your convolutions are purely verbal: at bottom, you are as simple and purely instinctive a creature as I." In so reducing the varieties of human nature, we not only do injustice to persons but diminish the width and depth of our vicarious experience.

Most critics and most readers would probably reject from the category of "great" literature any poetry which they deemed insincere. Yet it is not easy to fix a criterion. Feeling? The subjective response commonly endorses only authors of temperaments and attitudes akin to our own. Biography? Recourse to the writer's life, his correspondence, and his recorded conversations can show whether or not his creative self coincided with his private personality. Yet, if concurrence is not discovered, who is to say that the self revealed in art is not the central self? A shy or sensitive person may continually, by adaptation to context, misrepresent himself in public and find candor possible only in his poetry, where symbolism or singing-robes may at once veil and reveal.

In Crashaw's case, extraliterary corroborations are few; but what is to be known of his life gives no ground for suspicion that his poetry is anything save an ingenuous expression of his deepest spirit. Nor is it credible that his rhetoric was insincere. From the beginning to the end of his career, it was natural for him to be rhetorical; he was naturally a craftsman and an artist. There existed for him no dichotomy between discipline and self-expression, either in religion or in poetry. To learn the instruments of his craft, the forms of his worship, the methods of his devotion was but to find the means of expressing himself.

Yet granted his sincerity, all is not granted. Fanatics may be and commonly are sincere; fools are too stupid to be successful at the trade of hypocrisy. Sincerity is rather a minimum essential than an ultimate value. It conceded, we must judge of competence, of range, of aberration or wisdom.

It is the temperament expressed in Crashaw's poetry which elicits dubiety, stricture, or repugnance. Many readers have, without stopping to analyze, felt

themselves in the presence of something sick or un-
manly. Recollected, the pages of Crashaw breathe a
cloying sweetness, a languorous perfume. Recollected, there recur the images of nests and breasts,
wounds and blood—images symbolizing the need for
retreat and protection, images identifying suffering
with joy. The infant sucking milk; the martyr swim-
ming in blood: in Crashaw the undeveloped and the
overripe seem concurrently present.

About Crashaw, one critic feels "at times that his
passion for heavenly objects is imperfect because it is
partly a substitute for human passion"; about him
another says that the "collocation of torture and
erotic emotion . . . occurs repeatedly in his poetry
from first to last." These comments assume—rightly,
I think—that the character of a poet, as conveyed by
his poetry, counts centrally in our final estimate of a
poet.[3]

The problem of interpretation is exacting, involv-
ing as it does the relation of sex to religion, of the
poet's conscious meaning to the altered or additional
significance which his work may have for a later time,
and of the poet's character to the value of his work.

Historically, we reconstruct Crashaw into the supreme representative of baroque poetry; yet when
we set him among his English contemporaries we are
struck by his comparative isolation. We recollect that
he drew his themes and his figures out of Counter-
Reformation poetry, hagiography, and mysticism,
that his originality had nothing to do with invention;

yet we are left with the unmistakable impression of a personality. How are these contraries to be reconciled?

The answer is that Crashaw was not a Seicento Italian. Reared a Puritan, he became a Catholic; an Englishman, he took as his spiritual heroine a Spanish saint, and found the models for his style not in Jonson and Donne but in Marino and the Jesuits. As it remains today, so the tone of English Catholicism was sober and austere. The attraction for Crashaw of poetry like Marino's and themes like that of St. Alexis and the Sacred Wounds may, therefore, be taken as personally representative. If his materials can all be paralleled, his selection and his emphases are his own.

To the question whether we have any right to read back into Crashaw such psychological patterns as must always have existed but were not so named by the science of his day, the answer must be that we cannot help it. The meaning of a poem is primarily the poet's, and it is the reader's primary business (though not necessarily his initial attention) to make out what (in terms of his time) the poet could have meant; but we cannot evacuate our minds of their wonted furniture nor the race-mind of its accumulations. Meaning is, and meanings accrue. Our work as critical readers is to effect what harmonization we can between the past and the present.[4] Our feeling about Crashaw's exaltation of suffering will have to take into account the whole Christian tradition with its paradoxical Beatitudes along with our present attitude toward patience and aggression, passivity and action. Von Hügel's assertion that religion should be "world-penetrating" as well as "world-fleeing" might well define the normal aspiration for humane virtue as well, and "masochism" becomes then the symbol of a nature inadequately developed, pathological by its lack.

Crashaw's is an intense, not a large or various nature. His poetry lacks the gamut, lacks the contrasts common in the writings of the great saints and mystics—the alternating aridities and refreshments, feelings of alienation from God and of union with Him. The moral drama appears but fleetingly: weakness is, for Crashaw, real; evil scarcely is. One has but to contrast him with a less brilliant poet, George Herbert, to feel his comparative inhumanity. Ignoring, despising, or incapable of the "middle way," he moved from the aesthetic to the ascetic. He knew what it is to be a child and a scholar and a wit and an artist, but he did not know what it is to be a man.

Surely religion ought to provide comfort, relief, and use for all sorts and conditions of men: if all men are to love God, it must be according to their natures and their needs. "The holy Magdalen changed her object only, not her passion." But it is at least as true that, if religion is more than anodyne or compensation, it must also satisfy needs still exigent when all their "human" requisitions of bed, board, friendship, and marriage have been fulfilled.

It must offer something which a good man still lacks, though he be young, rich, and a ruler. The greatest saints, I should think, have, like the greatest poets, been "rich young rulers," not wanting for any of the ordinary ingredients of happiness, but still lacking, still desiring more—utterance, creation, the wisdom which comes from union with that which is known and adored.

There are poets to whom, without much strain of adaptation or adjustment of posture, one can always turn: Dante and Shakespeare among the great, Herbert and Marvell and Frost among the smaller. Their poetry, whether secular or Christian, is the expression of normal natures abnormally endowed with articulate imagination. Such art is no compensation for the poet's maladjustment or defect: it is sheer gratuity. Crashaw's was not such a nature and his is not such a poetry. On the other hand, both in manner and attitude, he is a traditionalist, though his tradition be that of Latin Europe, not that of Protestant England. His poetry flows from no self-conscious assertion of originality or "difference," no rebellion, no individualism.

Undoubtedly he gained by his adhesions. A "pure" artist, he was not an inventor of themes nor a thinker. His native impulse was undoubtedly frameless and inorganic—for the rosary of metaphors, for orchestration of some preëxistent melody, for decoration of some supplied vaulting. Catholic dogma afforded a system of doctrine implicit in his work and offered a degree of intellectual vertebration to poetry which would otherwise have lacked it.[5] Indeed, it is when one compares Crashaw's poetry with that of Poe, to which it has temperamental affinity, that one feels the gain to Crashaw's poetry from the culture in which it developed: it has more resonance than Poe's; it is not so monotonous; it is not provincial; it implies prospects larger than its own—European culture and Catholic Christendom.

Its special domain is not that of mountain and ocean nor yet of shop and home. It is the world of man's inner life at its mystical intensity, the world of devotion expressing itself through the sacraments and ceremonial and liturgy; it is a world which knows vision and rapture, tears and fire; it is a world of the supernatural, wherein the miraculous becomes the probable; and this world manifests itself to the senses in a rhetoric brilliant, expressive, and appropriate.

The light passes through colored and storied glass and flickers from high candles; it illuminates an altar of purple marble, surmounted by a triptych in polychrome and gold; a high mass is in celebration. Below the high thin voices of boys, the organ rumbles thickly. The air is redolent of rich, sharp incense. High above the chancel, the rood beam exhibits, in bold relief, the Crucified Lord and His suffering Mother; and in the church below, there is the dusky figure of one praying and adoring.

NOTES

CHAPTER ONE

1. The High Anglican doctrines and practices are best self-expounded in Andrewes' *Ninety-Six Sermons* and *Devotions*; Laud's *Conference with Fisher*; Cosin's *Works* (especially *Regni Angliae Religio Catholica* [IV, 339 ff.]) and *Correspondence*; Richard Montagu's *Apello Caesarem*; and Shelford's *Five Discourses*.

   The Puritan attack on the same doctrines and practices is most fully and readably to be found in Prynne's *Canterburies Doome* and other writings; cf. also John White's *First Century of Scandalous, Malignant Priests*.

   Excellent modern studies of the conflict between Laudians and Puritans are those by Hutton, Wakeman, and Carter.

2. Prynne, *Canterburies Doome*, 193; Hutton, *Laud*, especially 26, 48, 144–52.

3. *Conference with Fisher*, ed. Simpkinson, xxx.

4. The reader of Prynne will find chronicled the exploits of these young zealots or, at least, the excited rumors to which their ritualistic innovations had given rise. Cf. *Canterburies Doome*, 194–95; and *A Quench-Coale*, 11.

5. Shelford, *Five Discourses*, 19.

6. "The principal and truly so called (as generally necessary to Salvation) are Baptism and The Lord's Supper. The other five . . . though they be sometimes called and have the name of Sacraments, yet have they not the like nature that the two principal and true sacraments have" (*Devotions*, D 4 and 5).

7. Shelford, *loc. cit.*
8. *Responsio ad Apologiam Card. Bellarmini* (1610), 13. Cf. Ottley, 203.
9. Baker MS (Harl. 7 o 33), VI, 199–200; Prynne, *Canterburies Doome*, 192–93; Cooper, *Annals*, III, 287. Sparrow's sermon was published in 1637.
10. Osmond, *Cosin*, 87.
11. The Laudians "will now stile themselves and be called of others only Preists, (so *Shelford* termed himselfe in the Title page of his unlearned Treatises, and many others have done in late printed sermons and Pamphlets . . ." (Prynne, *A Quench-Coale*, 208).
12. Wren's inscription upon Andrewes' tomb in Southwark Cathedral says: *Coelebs hinc migravit ad aureolam coelestem*; Teale (*Lives of English Divines*, 82) explains that the aureole is the coronet which, according to ecclesiastical usage, is the reward of virgins. Cf. Macleane, *Lancelot Andrewes and the Reaction*, 184; and Taylor, *Holy Living* (15th ed., 1690), 73–75, 142.
13. G. C. Broderick, *History of the University of Oxford* (1886), 118.
14. *The Femall Glory* (4th ed.), 115–16, 177.
15. Hutton, *op. cit.*, 153–56.
16. Panzani, *Memoirs*, ed. Berington, 163; and Albion, *Charles I and the Court of Rome*, 145–92.
17. Albion, *op. cit.*, xii.
18. Helen C. White, *English Devotional Literature*, chap. VI, "Recusant Devotional Books in England," pp. 131 ff.
19. *Exomologesis*, 641 and 635–36. Cressy became the spiritual disciple of the great English mystic, Augustine Baker, whose *Sancta Sophia* he edited.
20. The frescoes of Pomarancio: Mâle, 110–12. The couplet is from Crashaw's "Hymn to . . . Sainte Teresa," Martin, 317.
21. Moeller, *Reformation and Counter-Reformation*, 218–75.
22. T. J. Campbell, *The Jesuits* (1921); and Füllöp-Miller, *The Power and Secret of the Jesuits*, tr. Flint and Tait (1930).

23. P. Guérin, *Les Petites Bollandistes Vies des Saints* (Paris, 1878), XIII, 178–95; XIV, 27–44.

24. St. Philip Neri: Newman, *The Idea of a University*, Discourse IX, sec. 9; Mâle, 153, 159–60.

    E. I. Watkin well writes: "If Bernini is Crashaw's counterpart in sculpture, assuredly St. Philip Neri was his prototype among the canonized saints. St. Philip passes long hours in his private oratory sipping the consecrated chalice, the Blood-Wine of Love—with such fervour and sweetness that his teeth have left their impress on the metal lip. So Crashaw" (*The English Way*, 283).

25. "Ces saints du moyen âge faisaient des miracles; les saints de la Contre-Réforme furent eux-mêmes des miracles" (Mâle, 152).

26. St. Teresa's *Interior Castle*, *passim*, but especially Mansion VI, caps. 3, 4, 6, 8. Cf. also Joly, *Psychology of the Saints*, 75, 79, 87.

27. *A Treatise of the Love of God*, tr. Thomas Carre (1630), Bk. VII, cap. 7.

CHAPTER TWO

1. The phrase quoted is from *The Honour of Vertue*, a memorial of the Rev. William Crashaw's second wife, who died in childbirth, October 8, 1620.

   The exact date of Richard Crashaw's birth has never been ascertained, and an investigation of such Puritan parish registers as those of St. Antholin and St. Mary Overy has proved vain. Presumably the poet was baptized at the Temple Church, of which his father was then rector; the extant records of this church begin only with 1628. What proximate evidence we have shall be cited.

   There is first the entry in the Admission Book of Pembroke, Cambridge, recording that, at his entry into that college on July 6, 1631, Crashaw was eighteen (*annos habens 18*); and the record of his death at Loreto on August 21, 1649, at which time he is said to have been "aetatis suae annorum 36 circiter"—about thirty-six years of age (Martin, 424).

Then in *The Honour of Vertue* we read: "The Funerall
Sermon was made by Doctor Usher of Ireland [later Archbishop of Armagh] then in England. . . . It was her own
earnest request to him, that he would preach at the Baptisme
of her Sonne, as he had eight years afore, being then also in
England, at the Baptisme of her husband's elder Sonne
[Richard]."

In 1603, Ussher was sent to London to buy books for
Trinity College, Dublin; in 1606, he again visited England;
and again in 1609. "After this he constantly came over into
England once in three years . . ." (Parr, *Life of Usher*
[1686]). On these triennial visits he made the acquaintance
of England's learned men, such as Bourchier, Camden, and
John Selden, who was a friend of William Crashaw; and it
is probable that it was also in 1609 that the learned young
Irishman and the learned preacher at the Temple Church
became acquainted. They and Thomas James, Bodley's
librarian, had a common interest in exposing "Romish
Forgeries and Falsifications" and in confuting Roman apolo-
gists.

Ussher's fourth stay in England can be dated, by means of
letters he wrote from London (*Works of Ussher*, XVI, 315–
21; XV, 72–75), as lasting from September, 1612 till April,
1613. "Eight years afore" his stepmother's funeral would
set Richard Crashaw's birth as October, 1612, but doubtless
this phrase will not bear too literal a reckoning.

2. THE LITERARY CAREER OF WILLIAM CRASHAW. For the ac-
quisition of books and learning, William Crashaw had a
passion: he describes himself, in a letter to the scholar-king,
James I, as having spent his patrimony in books and his
time in perusing them, and, in a letter to Casaubon, as
"totus . . . libris deditus et devotus." To the truth of these
avowals his preserved correspondence attests.

When, in 1614, he began a series of negotiations designed
to relieve his book-poor estate and to enrich the library of
his college, he wrote to Dr. Gwyn, then Master of St. John's,
that he had for disposal three thousand volumes and some
five hundred manuscripts. By 1615, he had already delivered

to Henry, Earl of Southampton, who purchased the books to present them to the College, nearly two hundred manuscripts in Greek, Latin, English, and French, and almost two thousand printed books. Though chiefly theological and ecclesiastical, the collection was rich, varied, and recondite. The manuscripts included Vergil, Statius, Ovid's *Metamorphoses*, the *Roman de la Rose*, Gower's works, St. Bernard's sermons on the *Song of Songs*, Richard Rolle's *Prick of Conscience*, the life of St. Catherine of Siena, the revelations of St. Bridget, the writings of Hugo and Richard of St. Victor.

The mention of these medieval and mystical manuscripts suggests that William Crashaw may have anticipated the devotional temper of his son. Such, however, was not the case. The father prodigiously collected Roman Catholic writings, both pre- and post-Tridentine, and in his will he declares himself "a member of the true Catholike churche," and a professor of "the Holy and Catholike faithe." But he hastens to add his denunciations of "Popery," as "the Heape and Chaos of all Heresies and the Channell wherein the fowlest impieties and heresies that have been in the Christian worlds have runne and closelye emptied themselves." In his *Jesuites Gospell* he proves the Pope to be Antichrist, sealed with the number of the Apocalyptic Beast, 666; and he avows elsewhere that, for aught we know, the true and absolute Papist debars himself from salvation.

His zeal for the study and collection of Catholic literature proceeded primarily from his polemics. Like many devout Protestants of his time, he was disturbed by that favorite taunt of the Roman Catholic controversialists—"Where was your church before Luther? Our church goes back to Christ and St. Peter; yours only to a renegade monk of the sixteenth century." The appeal to antiquity moved William Crashaw. Although a nineteenth-century Protestant would have thought it sufficient to show that his religion was that of the Scriptures and the Apostolic Age, Crashaw sought to prove more: he desired to establish the continuity of his own faith from the primitive Church down to his own time, proving that the chief doctors and commentators, though made in later editions of their texts to speak for—at least not against—Tridentine doctrine, had really witnessed against the corrupt belief of Roman doctrine.

Crashaw's *Romish Forgeries and Falsifications: Together with Catholike* [i.e., *Anglican*] *Restitutions*, issued in 1606, addressed a dedicatory epistle to the societies of the Two Temples, which he terms "the most comfortable and delightful company for a scholler, that (out of the Universities) this Kingdome yields." In the epistle he applied himself to answering that bitter taunt, "Where was your church before Luther?" Our religion, he contends, is the ancient faith of Christ and His Apostles, and has never ceased to be taught in all ages, by more or fewer. Many of the most learned theologians, such as Erasmus, Vives, Cajetan, Ferus, and Stella, agreed with Luther's chief doctrines. But when we turn to recent editions of these authors, we find them expurgated or altered.

The volume, offered as the First Book of the First Tome, is devoted to a specimen comparison of St. John's First Epistle. The variations between the texts receive detailed comment, and some dire betrayal of the truth is everywhere discovered. When the reason for the change is not patent, the exegete falls back on his faith in the pervasive cunning of Papists. "Here are also," he observed in one place, "the words [et baptisma] in what policie, or to what purpose I can not readily conjecture, but if it were well sifted there lyeth poyson under it: for *Deus et natura Romani pontificis nihil faciunt frustra.*"

Crashaw's projected exposure of papal censorship, planned on a vast scale, never reached further publication. But the cause remained his dominating intellectual passion; and he was forever collecting, and endeavoring to collect, the necessary documents. He begged Casaubon to urge upon King James the purchase of five hundred volumes, expressing the fear that the Jesuits would acquire the collection. He wrote the Earl of Salisbury, requesting a copy of each of the popish books recently seized by the state. Further, he addressed him-

self directly to the King, promising that, with the royal assistance, he could prove five thousand passages corrupted in
the writers of the last two hundred years.

Crashaw's other publications proceeded from the same
motives: hatred of Rome and the Jesuits, defense of the
Catholicity and continuity of the Reformed religion. For
example, he published in 1608 a free English version of
Balbani's *Historia della Vita di Galiacius Caracciolus* entitled *Newes from Italy* (in subsequent editions, *The Italian
Convert*). This book, which Archbishop Bancroft ordered
him to retract, chronicles, in a spirit of priggery and prudery,
the life story of an Italian marquis who abandoned his
ancestral faith, bade farewell to his wife, children, and aged
father, and departed for Geneva, where he enjoyed the
favor of Calvin and preached for the Italian congregation.
The tale is spiced with passing thrusts at monks and priests,
especially the Jesuits.

The *Jesuites Gospell* (1610) comprises Bonarscius' Latin
poem, addressed to the Virgin of Halle and the Child Jesus,
an English translation of this by William Crashaw, and the
translator's horrified exposition of the Jesuit poem. The
Mariolatric theme was to attract the son as it had repelled
the father; indeed, the whole poem anticipates the style of
Richard Crashaw: it antithesizes—and analogizes—the milk
of Mary and the blood of Christ:

> But ah, I thirst; ah, droght my breath doth smother,
> Quench me with blood, sweet Son; with milk, good
>   mother . . .
> Ah, when shall I with these be satisfi'd?
> When shall I swimme in joys of brest and side?
> . . . .
> I am better than thy nailes; yet did a streame
> Of thy dere blood wash both the lance and them.
> More worthy I than clouts; yet them a flood
> Moistened of mother's milk and of Son's blood. . . .

In 1611, Crashaw produced his closest approach to a devotional book, *A Manuall for True Catholickes*. Reiterating

prefatorily that our forefathers were "not of the Romish faith, but of our Religion," and that appearance to the contrary is of Romish craft, he assembles prayers, hymns, and creedal confessions designed to establish his contention as well as fortify the Reformed devout.

The *Manuall* includes Latin poems of approved piety and orthodoxy, with accompanying English versions by the compiler, versions conscientiously faithful to the sense of the original, but clumsy in versification. Nowhere, indeed, save in his version of Bonarscius, does he show himself a poet. His verses, customarily, are so much pious doggerel. The "ideas" may have attracted him, but he shows no feeling for rhythm or language—none of his son's extraordinary sensibility.

Crashaw's will, a lengthy document, assigned bequests of his rare books to the libraries of St. John's College, of the two universities, of Trinity College, Dublin, and others. Characteristically, however, most of the will is given over to a final recital of Crashaw's faith, more eloquent and more moving than anything he had published. "And all other names of salvation I utterlye renounce Cleavinge only to the blessed and all sufficient merritts and Blood sheddinge of Jesus Christ In the arms of whose mercye stretched oute uppon the Crosse to receive me and all true penitent Synners I leave this poore and otherwise succourless Soule of myne whome all the Relicks in Rome and all the meritts of Saincts in the Popes Treasurye are not able to helpe with one dramme of true comfort But of him throughe him and for him is my salvation Therefore to him be glorye in my lyfe and deathe and forever and ever Amen."

For William Crashaw's library, cf. four of his letters, *The Eagle* of St. John's, Cambridge, XXIII (1901), 22–25; M. R. James, *Descriptive Catalogue of Manuscripts in the Library of St. John's College Cambridge* (1913), vi–viii. At the British Museum, there are letters and other Crashaviana: Cotton MS, Julius C. III, 126; Add. MS, 12, 497, f. 467; Add. MS, 5 865, f. 28; Add. MS 17,083, f. 145 b; Royal MS 17,B.9 ("A Discovery of Popish Corruption,"

addressed to King James). The will, from which I quote, is
at Somerset House (Prerogative Court of Canterbury, Regis-
ter 97 Hele).

3. Archives of the See of Westminster (MSS Archiv. Westmon.,
Vol. XXX, No. 100). Quoted by Martin, xxxiv, n.

4. Lloyd, *Memoires* . . . , 618.

5. Davies, *Charterhouse*, 201–4 and 249–50.

6. *Ibid.*, 207–8, 253–59.

7. Lloyd, *loc. cit.*; Crashaw's "Ornatissimo viro Praeceptori
suo colendissimo, Magistro Brook," prefixed to *Epigrammata
Sacra* (Martin, 10), and a dedication, in prose and verse,
written for the same book but rejected (Martin, 368).

8. Watson, *English Grammar Schools*, chaps. xxiv ("The Mak-
ing of Latins"), xxvi ("Theme Writing"), and xxvii
("The Teaching of Rhetoric"); and Wallerstein, *Richard
Crashaw*, 60–72.

9. Herne, *Domus Carthusiana*, 137; Lloyd, *loc. cit.*

10. Herne, *op. cit.*, 187–88. The "exhibition" amounted, in
Crashaw's time, to twenty pounds a year. The entry in the
Admission Book of Pembroke College reads: "Julii 6. 1631.
Richardus Crashawe Gulielmi pr[e]sbyteri filius natus
Londini annos ha[b]ens 18, admissus est ad 2^{ae} mensae
ordinem sub tutela M^{ri} Tourney."

11. Cf. Warren, "Crashaw's *Epigrammata Sacra*," *Journal of
English and Germanic Philology*, XXXIII, 233 ff., especially
pp. 234–35 and note. Shortly after I had published the
article, the late Aubrey Attwater, then Librarian of Pembroke, discovered, and sent me, Matthew Wren's digest of
the Statutes of the Watt Foundation, upon which I have
based my account of the Greek Scholarship.

The statute prescribing the composition of sacred epigrams
reads: "To make verses. 4 Hexam. Pentam. Latin as many
Greeks of ye same matter at Circumcision, Epiphany, Purification [of the Blessed Virgin], Annunciation, Easter, Ascension, Pentecost, Trinity Sun, All Sts, Xtmas, Good friday.
2 greeke 2 Latin e'ry Sunday other holy day. Written wth
theire owne hand, set on ye skreene before dinner. The
argument of ye verses to be taken out of some pt of ye

Scriptures yt day read. To have 7ˢ 5d a yeare payd by quart's for verses."

12. Laney, *Five Sermons* (1669); Attwater, *Pembroke College*, 70 ff.; and *DNB*. Extruded from his mastership by the Puritans, Laney remained zealously loyal to the Stuarts; and, after the Restoration, he was rewarded by successive appointments to the sees of Peterborough, Lincoln, and Ely.

It has been supposed by Grosart (*Works of Crashaw*, II, xli), and by others, following him, that B. L., who wrote the verses, "A Conclusion to the Author and his Booke," appended to William Crashaw's *Manuall for True Catholickes*, was Laney; hence, that the Master of Pembroke had earlier been Puritan in his sympathies and that, for Richard, the "transition between the grim Puritanism of his father's household and the fervid Anglicanism of Cambridge was made easy . . . by the personal character and guidance" of Laney. These suppositions rest on nothing more than the conjecture of the nineteenth-century antiquary, Joseph Hunter (*Chorus Vatum*, 38 v.), that B. L. "may possibly be B. Leo, or Benjamin Lany. . . ."

13. Martin, 2–3 and 6–8. Grosart translates the printed preface (II, 11–15).

14. Cooper's *Annals*, III, 263–64; Martin, 208–9 and 425–26. Cf. also Attwater, *op. cit.*, 70. "Venerabili viro Magistro Tournay," *ibid.*, 9.

15. Mullinger, *University of Cambridge*, II, 372 ff.; III, 67.

16. Martin, 384–88.

17. *Ibid.*, 14 and xxii. I quote, slightly altered, the translation of Grosart (*op. cit.*, II, 32–33).

18. The prose is my translation from "Epitaphium in Dominum Herrisium" (Martin, 164); the verse is from "Upon the Death of the most desired Mr. Herrys" (*ibid.*, 168). What suggests that Crashaw's poems on Herrys may be expressions of personal grief rather than ceremonial performances is less their tone than their number: the death of a youthful Fellow, even of one's own college, scarcely requires the composition of five elegies.

19. A complete list of these commemorative anthologies is to be

found in R. Bowes' *Catalogue of Books* . . . , Cambridge, 1894.

Miss Wallerstein (*Crashaw*, 26) argues convincingly that Crashaw is the "R. C." who contributed a Latin elegy to the *Justa Edouardo King Naufrago*, the 1637 volume which included "Lycidas."

20. Martin, 156.
21. Cf. Warren, "Crashaw's Paintings at Cambridge," *Modern Language Notes*, XLVIII, 365–66.

Carmen Deo Nostro, published after Crashaw's death, contains twelve engravings; and its editor's introductory epigram acclaims "the pictures in the following Poemes which the Authour first made with his owne hand, admirably well, as may be seene in his Manuscript dedicated to the right Honorable Lady the L. Denbigh." Of these engravings, two are simple emblems: a padlocked heart, and a bust of the Magdalen behind a bleeding heart tipped with a flame and winged; a third reproduces, from a papal coin, the *impresa* of Urban VI; some of the remainder, far more elaborate, bear the name of Jean Messager, the French engraver.

L. C. Martin, in discussing these pictures (*Crashaw*, xlviii), represents Thomas Carre as wishing posterity to believe that Crashaw designed them all; but Carre's sentence is susceptible of another—and more plausible—reading. It would appear that Crashaw made a holograph version of the *Carmen*, which he presented to his patroness, Lady Denbigh. In substitution for the illuminations of a medieval manuscript, he adorned his with vignettes copied, for the most part, from existing engravings, and probably colored. When the book was subsequently published, the engravings which Crashaw had copied were inserted at the appropriate positions. The two simple emblems were undoubtedly of Crashaw's own composition; they, and possibly that of the coin, are surely the only engravings made expressly for the volume.

22. He translated from Vergil's *Georgics* (Martin, 155), Catullus (194), and Horace (382); from Martial (188), Pe-

tronius (382), and Ausonius (161); from the *Greek Anthology* (161), Heliodorus (158), and Moschus ("Idyll I" [159]); from Barclay (338 and 392), Grotius (*Christus Patiens* [398]), Strada (149), and Hermannus Hugo (381).

23. Cf. Warren, "Crashaw's *Epigrammata Sacra,*" *Journal of English and Germanic Philology*, XXXIII, 236–38.

24. Martin, 183 and note (the printed title is "To the Morning. Satisfaction for sleepe"); and *ibid.*, 221 ("Woman the treasury of evils").

25. Epigram "On Marriage" (*ibid.*, 183).

26. For evidence, cf. "Crashaw's Residence at Peterhouse," London *Times Literary Supplement*, Nov. 3, 1932.

27. John Hutchinson, *Memoirs* (ed. C. H. Firth, 1885), I, 72–74.

28. Wren's career was abruptly stopped by the Civil War; the Puritans, who despised him as "a notable craftie insinuating fellow" (*Wren's Anatomy*, 2–3), and a zealous Laudian, shut him up in the Tower, where he remained for upwards of seventeen years. Puritan diatribes against him are *The Wren's Nest defil'd . . .* , 1641, and *Wren's Anatomy discovering his notorious pranks . . .* , 1644. For Wren's services to Pembroke College, cf. Attwater, *op. cit.*, 65 ff.

It was a common charge against the Laudians that they attacked—and neglected—preaching, in reply to which they charged the Puritans with an inordinate passion for hearing sermons, to the neglect of prayer and praise. Cosin at Brancepeth and Ferrar at Little Gidding erected pulpit and reading desk of equal height, in order to show that prayer should be considered an ordinance of equal value with preaching (Osmond, 20; Carter, 111; cf. also Shelford, 12).

29. Osmond, *Cosin*, 18 and 70; cf. also Cosin's *Correspondence*, I, 161–69, for the "Articles . . . against Cosin, Burgoine, Blaxton, Hunt, Lindsell, James . . . all learned clerks of the cathedrall Church of Durham."

30. *Canterburies Doome*, 73.

Thomas Walker reprints (*Peterhouse*, 207–10) a record in Cosin's handwriting of donors to the completion of the chapel and of furnishings purchased—e.g., "Vasa et ornatus Altaris locique circumjacentis," "Pavimentum marmore polito stratum," "Vestimenta et stragulae phrygiae," "Frontispicium Altaris de marmore polito," "Pallium cum frontalibus holosericis."

31. Mullinger, *op. cit.*, III, 141–42.

32. Martin, 206–8.

33. *Works of Ussher*, ed. Elrington, XVI, 9.

34. "On a Treatise of Charity" (Martin, 137–39 and note). The lines last quoted were dropped from the poem as given in *Steps to the Temple*, probably by the action of an editor unwilling to give needless offense. Even the Laudians were not agreed on their attitude toward Rome and the Pope, some, like Ferrar, continuing to believe him Antichrist. By 1635 Crashaw had discarded this dogma dear to his father.

35. My account of Little Gidding and its founder is based chiefly on Peckard's *Memoirs of the Life of Mr. Nicholas Ferrar* (1790), and *Nicholas Ferrar, His Household and his Friends*, ed. by the Rev. T. T. Carter (1893).

36. Several of the Harmonies are now in the British Museum (Bibl. Reg. C23, e², e³, e⁴). There, also, is the manuscript (Add. MS 34657–9) of "Religious Conversations at Little Gidding," from which Miss Sharland drew her *Story Books*.

37. Carter, chap. VI, "The Maiden Sisters," 132 ff.

38. Cf. *The Arminian Nunnery* . . . (London, 1641). Isaak Walton, *Lives of Donne, Wotton, Hooker, Herbert, and Sanderson*, ed. Bullen (1884), 315.

39. To a translation of *Hygiasticon* (1634), Crashaw contributed verses "In praise of Lessius his rule of health" (Martin, 156). The translation was made by Ferrar's relative, Thomas Sheppard (cf. London *Times Literary Supplement*, June 7 and 28; July 5, 1917), and Crashaw's connection with the book makes it probable that he was already, by 1634, a visitor to Little Gidding.

Of the Ferrar vigils, Peckard wrote (*op. cit.*, 243): "Several religious persons both in the neighbourhood, and from distant places, attended these watchings; and amongst these the celebrated Mr. Rich. Crashaw, Fellow of Peterhouse, who was very intimate in the family, and frequently came from Cambridge for this purpose, and at his return often watched in Little St. Mary's Church near Peterhouse."

40. Walker, *Admissions to Peterhouse*, 55. In the whole course of Crashaw's fellowship, but six students were committed to his care; and of these, three were subsequently transferred to other tutors.

41. Mullinger, *History of the University of Cambridge*, 117; Walker, *Peterhouse*, 188.

42. Crashaw was probably ordained by Matthew Wren, Cosin's predecessor as Master of Peterhouse and, since 1638, Bishop of Ely, the diocese which includes Cambridge; but the records of Ely ordinations during this period no longer exist.

This and the following five paragraphs summarize my documented article, "Richard Crashaw, Catechist and Curate," *Modern Philology*, XXXII, 261–69.

43. The authority for this paragraph is the unsigned preface to *Steps to the Temple*. The identity of its writer remains obscure: Martin (432) conjectures him to be some member of the community at Little Gidding; I should suppose him to be Joseph Beaumont, Crashaw's close friend, of whose florid prose style there exist not dissimilar specimens. Because "Tertullian's roofe of Angels" is assigned to Little St. Mary's, and because Cosin's celebrated sculptured angels adorned the Peterhouse chapel, it has been said that the prefacer was unfamiliar with Cambridge; but such a confusion would have been as impossible for a Ferrar as for Beaumont, and I take the "angels" to be the imagined guardians of any church rather than effigies set up by a Laudian.

44. Martin, 220–21. Italics are mine. On Crashaw's poem, I follow the interpretation of Canon Beeching (the "Muses Library" *Crashaw*, xxviii and note). Nethercot (*Cowley*, 43–44) agrees.

45. The oration is to be found in a manuscript volume, "A Collection of my R[evd]. Father's Latin Speeches," presented to the library of Peterhouse by the Master's son.

46. John Gee, who prefixed an "Account of the Life and Writings of the Author" to his edition of Beaumont's *Original Poems in Latin and English* (Cambridge, 1749), printed for the first time "De Legendis Sanctorum Historiis Dissertatio" (pp. 107–17).

47. *Minor Poems of Joseph Beaumont*, ed. Robinson, 275, 260, 253.

48. In the Fourth Canto of his *Psyche*, Beaumont assembles his favorite bards. As lyric poets, he praises Pindar, Horace, and George Herbert; as epic poets, Homer, Vergil, Tasso, and Spenser. Then follows a stanza in eulogy of St. Gregory of Nazianzen, the great fourth-century poet of the Eastern Church; and this leads to Crashaw, for—

> by this heart-attracting Pattern [St. Gregory] Thou
> *My only worthy Self* thy songs didst frame:
> Witness those polished *Temple Steps* which now
> Stand as the ladder to thy mounting fame;
>   And spight of all thy Travels, mak't appear
>   Th'art more in England than when Thou wert here.
>
> More unto others, but not so to me
> Privy of old to all thy secret Worth;
> What half-lost I endure for want of *Thee*,
> The World will read in this mishapen *Birth*.
>   Fair had my *Psyche* been, had she at first
>   By thy judicious hand been drest and nurst.

49. Walker, *Peterhouse*, 107–8; and Martin, 418–91.

50. Cooper, *op. cit.*, III, 364–66.

51. *Querela Cantabrigiensis*, 13–15.

52. Warren, "Crashaw's Residence at Peterhouse," London *Times Literary Supplement*, Nov. 3, 1932.

53. Warren, "Crashaw, Catechist and Curate," *Modern Philology*, XXXII, 265 and note.

54. This, the only letter of Crashaw's known to exist, was first published by E. C. Sharland in her "Richard Crashaw and Mary Collet," *Church Quarterly Review*, LXXIII (1912), 358, and has been reprinted by Martin (xxvii–xxxi). I

find convincing—and follow—Martin's interpretation of the letter.

In 1632, Mrs. Ferrar resigned her post as director of Little Gidding's women, and her granddaughter, Mary Collett, was elected to succeed her under the title of "Mother" (Carter, *op. cit.*, 147, 162–63). Miss Collett did not die in Paris (as Shorthouse, in *John Inglesant*, that sensitive re-creation of the seventeenth century and its spiritual life, has her do), but survived Little Gidding and Cromwell, living till 1682.

55. Warren, "Crashaw's 'Apologie,'" London *Times Literary Supplement*, Nov. 16, 1935.

56. MS volume of Beaumont's sermons in the library of Peterhouse. The discourse from which I quote was preached on January 30, the anniversary of King Charles' martyrdom.

57. *Fasti Oxonienses* (1691), II, col. 688 (Martin, 417).

58. Martin, 417 and xxxiii.

59. Albion, *Charles I and the Court of Rome,* "Converts at Court," 193–215; Haynes, *Henrietta Maria*, chap. v ("The Queen's Converts") and chap. x ("The Queen of the Exiles").

60. Dodd, *Church History of England*, III, 305; Gillow, II, 506–9; Albion, 197–98.

61. The fullest account of Carre and his community of nuns is that of Abbé F. M. Cédoz, *Un Couvent de Religieuses Anglaises à Paris* (Paris, 1891). Cf. also Dodd, III, 17–20.

62. Richard Watson, *The Rt. Rev. Dr. J. Cosin . . . His Opinion . . . for Communicating rather with Geneva than Rome . . .* (1684), 15. Cf. "Crashaw and Peterhouse," London *Times Literary Supplement*, August 13, 1931.

63. On the Queen and Crashaw, cf. Nethercot, *op. cit.*, 98–99; Haynes, *op. cit.*, 221–22; *Legenda Lignea*, cxxxviii; Dodd, *op. cit.*, 303.

64. *The Flaming Hart*, a translation of the *Vida* published at Antwerp in 1642, was dedicated to the Queen: to St. Teresa "already you carry an extraordinary devotion; and not only devotion to her selfe, but affection also, to the holy Religious woemen of her Angelicall Order. . . ."

65. Hutton, *William Laud*, 144; Haynes, *op. cit.*, 137; E. E. Phare, "The Conversion of Crashaw's Countess of Denbigh," *Cambridge Review*, Dec. 2, 1932, 147–49.

66. Phare, *op. cit.*, 148.

67. Carre, "très amateur de livres, avait également une remarquable habileté en peinture, en gravure sur cuivre, en sculpture" (Cédoz, 111).

68. This and the preceding quotation of verse are from Carre's anagram on the name of Crashaw (Martin, 233–34).

69. I translate the Queen's French (Haynes, *op. cit.*, 328).

70. Von Ranke, *History of the Popes of Rome*, tr. E. Foster (London, 1876), II, 263–67, 321–29. Von Pastor, *Geschichte der Päpste zeit dem Ausgang des Mittelalters* (1899–1933), XIII, 248–63, and 882–980 ("Literarischer und Künstlerischer Mäzenat Urbans VIII"); XIV, 23–38.

71. Martin, xxxiv–xxxv.

72. Bargrave, *Pope Alexander the Seventh and the College of Cardinals*, 34–37; also H. C[ogan] (tr.), *The Scarlet Gown, or the History of all the Present Cardinals of Rome* . . . (London, 1653), 78–83. Under Urban VIII, Pallotta was Lord Governor of Rome, "Wherein he carried himself with much integrity, and to the great satisfaction of the people, being severe and so upright, that in point of justice he made no reckoning of his Holiness Nephewes." "His Votes, as well in the Congregation, as in the Consistory, are greatly esteemed: He hath no Enemy, nor any that is contrary to him: He honors all, and where he can do any service, he doth it willingly: he is affable in entertainment, leades a holy and retired life, loves not light conversations, and is very studious" (*The Scarlet Gown*).

73. Bargrave, *op. cit.*, 34–37. "When I went first of my four times to Rome," says Bargrave, "there were four revolters to the Roman Church that had been fellows of Peterhouse in Cambridge with myself." The three other converts were Francis Blakiston, Christopher Bankes, and Richard Nichols.

74. H. Torsellinus, S. J., *The History of our B. Lady of Loreto*, tr. T. Price; and G. E. Phillips, *Loreto and the Holy House*.

75. Phillips, *op. cit.*, 159–63.
76. Martin, xxxvii–xxxviii and 420–24.
77. "On the Death of Mr. Crashaw," *The Works of Mr. Abraham Cowley* (10th ed., 1707), I, 44–47.
78. No portrait of Crashaw is known to exist. His memorial-window in the Combination Room at Peterhouse, designed by Ford Madox-Brown and reproduced as frontispiece of Vol. II of Grosart's large-paper edition of *The Complete Works*, is an imaginary if artfully apt conception: Crashaw wears the vestments of a priest; in one hand he holds a copy of *Carmen Deo Nostro*, in the other a palette and brushes; and just behind his laureled head hovers the Holy House of Loreto, sustained by angels.

CHAPTER THREE

1. My characterization of baroque art is based chiefly upon three masterly books: Mâle's *L'Art Religieux après le Concile de Trente*; G. Scott's *The Architecture of Humanism*; and Wölfflin's *Principles of Art History*. Copious reproductions of the ecclesiastical architecture, painting, and sculpture are to be found in C. Ricci's *Baroque Architecture and Sculpture in Italy* (London, 1912); G. Magni's *Il Barocco a Roma e nella Scultura decorativa* (Turin, 1911)—of which Vol. I is devoted to churches; A. E. Brinckmann's *Barockskulptur* . . . (Berlin, 1919); and W. Pinder's *Deutsche Barock-plastik* (Leipzig, 1933); cf. also W. Hausenstein's fully illustrated *Vom Geist des Barock* (Munich, 1924).
2. Mâle, chap. I, "L'art et les artistes après le concile de Trente," especially pp. 15–17.
3. *Ibid.*, chap. III, "Le Martyre," especially pp. 116–26.
4. *Ibid.*, chap. V, "La Mort," especially pp. 220–21.
5. *Ibid.*, chap. IV, "La Vision et l'extase."
6. The Jesuits "furent les premiers probablement à faire peindre sur la voûte de la nef un ciel qui la fit disparaître" (Mâle, *op. cit.*, 197–98). Cf. Hausenstein, plates 48–50.
7. Burckhardt, *The Civilization of the Renaissance in Italy*, Part V, chap. VIII, "The Festivals."
8. *Exercitia Spiritualia*, I Hebdomada, Exercitium quintum.

9. "In meditatione de re invisibili, ut est hic de peccatis, compositio erit videre visu imaginationis et considerare animam meam esse in hoc corpore corruptibili tamquam carcere inclusam, et totum compositum in hoc valle tamquam exsulans inter bruta animalia" (I Hebdomada, Exercitium primum).

10. Füllöp-Miller, *The Power and Secret of the Jesuits,* illustrations opp. pp. 6 and 7.

11. Praz, *Studi sul Concettismo,* 42.

12. *Ibid.,* 134–35.

13. "To the Reader," *Emblemes,* 1635.

14. Praz, *op. cit.,* 105.

15. *Ibid.,* chap. IV, "L'utile e il dolce" (on the Jesuit employment of the *impresa* and the emblem), especially pp. 135–39, 158–62.

16. The representative volumes I describe are all in the Widener Library at Harvard, which has an excellent collection of emblematists.

17. Praz, "The English Emblem Literature," *English Studies,* XVI (1934), 129–40.

18. *School of the Heart,* Epigram 10.

19. The design might prompt a longer poem as well as an epigram; and, with Quarles, it often does, especially if the design be elaborate. Emblem 14 of Book III depicts the Body (a naked and fleshly female) turning her back upon the prospect in order to look through a prism at the shifting colors of appearances, while, seated by her, the modestly garbed Soul peers intently through a telescope at the realities, a skeletal Death and a triangular Trinity. To develop the design requires a lyric of some length.

20. "The aim of the poet is the marvelous. . . . He who knows not how to astonish deserves the cudgel!" *La Murtoleide,* Fischiata 33 (Marino, *Poesie Varie,* ed. Croce [Bari, 1913], 395).

CHAPTER FOUR

1. On the epigram and its history, cf. J. C. Scaliger, *Poetices* . . . (1561), Bk. III, cap. 126; J. Pontanus, *Poeticarum*

Institutionum . . . (1600), Bk. III, caps. 1–13; N.
Mercier, *De Conscribendo Epigrammata* (1653); J. Booth,
Epigrams Ancient and Modern (2nd ed., 1865); T. K.
Whipple, *Martial and the English Epigram* (1925).

2. "Salves rather than wounds are the wounds of Christ; for by
His stripes He heals our wounds." Owen, *Epigrammata*, Bk.
III, no. 94; *ibid.*, Bk. III, nos. 62, 63, and 53. There is a
faithful if uninspired translation of Owen's epigrams by
Thomas Harvey (London, 1677).

The epigrams of the Cantabrigian Benlowes have striking
analogies to those of Crashaw; and *Sphinx Theologica*—
which is variously dated as 1626 and 1636—shows that
Benlowes knew the Jesuit epigrammatists, as his *Theophila*
(Saintsbury, *Minor Caroline Poets*, I, 307 ff.) shows that
he knew the Continental mystics.

Martin (424–30) in his sequence of parallels to Crashaw's
celebrated verse, "Nympha pudica Deum vidit, et erubuit"
(*ibid.*, 38), does not cite Benlowes' "Conversio Aquae in
Vinum" (*Sphinx*, 51):

> Candida Lympha fuit, sed et illa rubescere coepit;
> Praecox mutata stellat Jacchus aqua.

> In mustum convertis aquas (mirabile!) fusas;
> Vinaque de nullo palmite nata fluunt.

> Sic sine vite Latex fit Nectar ovantis Jacchi.
> Coelitus ille latex ebrius: inde rubet.

3. "The Magdalen and Afra occupy a common canvas—the one
with her tears, the other with her fire. Why, painter, do you
put contraries into the same painting, and place wet streams
next flames? It is so permitted, lest the depicted Afra should
be consumed by her fire, that the depicted Magdalen should
join to the other her waters." Biderman, *Epigrammatum*
. . . (Venice, 1711), 133.

4. "Venturing to snare God with those unloosed tresses by which
she snares mortal lovers, while the Magdalen is casting her
golden nets over the sacred feet, the preyer becomes the

prey of her own prey." Bettinus, *Florilegium* (1632), 79; *ibid.*, 79 and 124.

5. Quintilian, *Institutiones Oratoriae*, Bk. VIII, cap. 6, and Bk. IX, caps. 1–3.

6. "Lectori," ll. 51–68 (Martin, 12). For a free translation, cf. Grosart's *Crashaw*, II, 25–27.

7. Warren, "Crashaw's *Epigrammata Sacra*," *Journal of English and Germanic Philology*, XXXIII (1934), 235–39.

8. Andrewes, *Seventeen Sermons on the Incarnation*, 29. Delivered on Dec. 25, 1606.

9. Martin, 16 (2) ["My life means your death"]; 21 (3) ["For Him there is no place without Whom there is no Place"]; 27 (2) ["She looks down, yet thus she sees Heaven"]; 16 (4) ["Food itself is fed"]; 41 (3); 41 (2) ["This was also to give: to refuse to give"]; 51 (1) ["It is bread not to have had bread"]; 90 (2).

10. *Ibid.*, 47 (4) ["The guard imposed chains, and thereby gave weapons"]; 22 (2) ["Reverse your art, and now you too learn to be caught"].

11. *Ibid.*, 33 (4) [translation by Barksdale]; 29 (1) ["Your shadow will enable me to see the sun; and thus my light will be the shade of your shade"].

12. *Ibid.*, 17 (3) ["Those fellows threw away; she gave"]; 26 (4) ["It feeds both the people's famine and their faith"].

13. *Ibid.*, 17 (2); 17 (4); 33 (1); 24 (1); 50 (1) ["Thirst is driven thence, but hence another thirst arises"].

14. *Ibid.*, 42 (4) ["That the earth trembles forbids you to doubt"]; 19 (2) ["And a shadow prevents your becoming ghosts"]; 31 (3); 36 (2) ["This, that one should be so borne, this also was to bear"]; 24 (3) ["the 'Milky Way' "].

357 (2) ["And now you lie open. The grievous spear has thrown back the bolt of the heart, and the nails, as keys, unlock all your quarters"]. St. Bernard had employed the same apt pun. "But the nail that pierced Him has been for us a key to unlock the mind of the Lord: *clavis reserans clavus penetrans factus est*" (*Sermons on the Canticle*, II, 198).

15. *Ibid.*, 15 (3) [Barksdale (1682) translates:

"See, O my kinsmen, what a strange thing is this!
Christ in's own country a great stranger is.
The thief which bled upon the Cross with Thee
Was more ally'd in consanguinity"].

In 1682 Clement Barksdale published *Epigrammata Sacra,
cum Anglica Versione*, a brochure reprinting (without acknowledgment of their author) forty-two of Crashaw's epigrams and adding English translations.

16. Martin, 30 (1) ["Give support; give a support to me: of
what sort? a cross"]; 25 (4) ["The Word in the midst of
the thorns"]; 31 (2); 54 (3).

17. *Ibid.*, 21 (2); 40 (1).

18. *Ibid.*, 41 (4) ["O too blooming with rosy lips"]; 40 (4)
["Blessed is the womb that bare Thee, and the paps which
Thou hast sucked"—Luke 11:27]; 37 (3).

19. In the *Journal of English and Germanic Philology*, XXXIII,
233–34, I have given an account of one such manuscript of
sacred epigrams.

20. Carew, "Spring," *Minor Poets of the 17th Century*, ed.
Howarth, 65.

21. Martin, *Crashaw*, 169.

22. Beaumont (*Psyche*, Canto IV, stanza 105) finds Spenser
"manacled in thick and peevish rhyme."

23. "His Discourse with Cupid," *The Poems of Ben Jonson*, ed.
Newdigate (1936), 93.

24. Martin, *op. cit.*, 175, 167–94.

25. *Ibid.*, 170.

26. *Ibid.*, 166, 183–85.

27. Cf. Campbell, "The Christian Muse," *Huntington Library
Bulletin*, VIII, 29–70.

28. Martin, 143–45. The Cowley-Crashaw dialogue, first published in 1646, was written when both poets were together
at Cambridge (cf. Nethercot, *Cowley*, 44–45); a much
altered version appeared in *Carmen Deo Nostro*.

29. Cf. Williamson, *The Donne Tradition*, 111–23.

30. Martin, 175.

31. "Upon Ford's two Tragedyes," Martin, 181. The two

tragedies are "Love's Sacrifice" and "The Broken Heart," both published in 1633.

32. Cf. *The Poetical Works of William Drummond of Hawthornden*, ed. L. E. Kastner (Edinburgh, 1913); and R. Wallerstein, "The Style of Drummond of Hawthornden in its Relation to his Translations," *Publications of the Modern Language Association*, XL (1933), 1090–1107. Drummond borrowed more largely from Marino than from any other Continental poet, and he was much influenced by Sidney, who in turn owed much to the Italians. In these respects, and in others, the parallel to Crashaw is obvious.

33. Ascham, *The Scholemaster* (1570), Bk. II.

34. The phrase comes from Dryden's Preface to *Sylvae* (1685).

35. This paragraph owes much to C. B. Mitchell's excellent thesis, *The Translations . . . of Richard Crashaw* (Wesleyan, 1929).

36. Martin, 188–89 and (for the Italian original) 442–43.

37. Strada's *Prolusiones*, a set of discourses on the method and style of oratory, history, and poetry, gives the fifth and sixth prolusions of the Second Book to conversations between such Renaissance men of letters as Pontanus, Castiglione, Hercules Strozza, Bembo, Naugerius, Parrhasius, and Sadoleto, in the course of which these distinguished humanists, each espousing the name and cause of a Roman poet, recite verses imitating the styles of Lucan, Lucretius, Claudian, Ovid, Statius, and Vergil.

38. Du Bartas, like Sandys, describes the nightingales as vying with one another:

> The first replyes, and descants thereupon;
> With divine warbles of Division,
> Redoubling Quavers; And so (turn by turn)
> Alternately they sing away the Morn:
> So that the conquest in this curious strife
> Doth often cost the one her voyce and life.

J. Sylvester, *Du Bartas his Divine Weekes and Workes* (London, 1621), 44–45. Sandys, "Upon the Sixth Book of Ovid's Metamorphosis," *Ovid* (1632), 227.

39. Hawkins, *Partheneia Sacra*, 139. John Dowland, the celebrated lutenist and composer, died *circa* 1626.
40. Strada's poem is given by Martin, 438–39; for "Music's Duel," cf. *ibid.*, 149–53.
41. Marino, *L'Adone*, Canto VII, stanzas 30–57.
42. "Music and Poetry are a pair of sisters" (*L'Adone*, Canto VII, stanza 1).
43. Here I differ with Miss Wallerstein (*Crashaw*, 39–40, 48–49, and *passim*). All that we know of Crashaw's "skill in musicke" is the bare mention of it by the prefacer of *Steps to the Temple*. Some of Joseph Beaumont's minor poems are inscribed "Sett for voices and violls by R. C.," and their editor, Miss Robinson (xv), conjectures that the composer may be Crashaw; but search has discovered none of these settings.

    Miss Wallerstein seems to assume that "musical" poetry is written by poets who are also musicians, but the case for such correlation is far from clear. Browning, for example, was a musician; Poe was not.
44. "Another Venus holds us, another Cupid. Assuredly, Love is here; here also is the Mother of Love; But the Mother is a Virgin, nor is the Love blind." For the Latin text, cf. Martin, 13.
45. Preface, *Steps to the Temple* (Martin, 75).
46. The figure was apparently originated by Thomas Fuller, who wrote of Quarles that he "drank of Jordan instead of Helicon, and slept on Mount Olivet for his Parnassus." *Worthies of England* (ed. Nuttall, 1840), I, 519. In his *Fragmenta Poetica* (1650), Nicholas Murford writes:

    > Therefore, Lord, I'll think on
    > Thy Jordan, for my purest Helicon;
    > And for bi-forked Parnassus, I will set
    > My fancy on Thy sacred Olivet.

47. Martin, 416.
48. *Christ's Victory and Triumph*, ed. W. T. Brooke, 24–25.
49. Cf. Warren, "George Herbert," *American Review*, VII, 249–71.

50. "The Crosse," Grierson's *Donne*, I, 331–33.
51. Southwell, *Poetical Works*, ed. Turnbull, 119, 68. Of Christ's circumcision, Southwell writes (112):

> Tears from His eyes, blood streams from wounded place,
> >   With showers to heaven of joy a harvest bring:
> This sacred dew let angels gather up,
> Such dainty drops best fit their nectar'd cup.

52. *Christ's Victory and Triumph*, 91, 110, 117.
53. *Ibid.*, 68, 67.
54. Cf. Praz, "Robert Southwell's 'St. Peter's Complaint' and its Source," *Modern Language Review*, XIX (1924), 273–90. My statement that Fletcher knew the Italian *concettists* rests upon internal evidence alone.
55. For Marino's life, cf. Cabeen's *L'Influence de G. Marino*, 7–19.
56. Marino, "witty in his Epigrams, epic in his *Adonis*, noble in his *Innocents*, in shorter poems worthy of the laurel." Cf. London *Times Literary Supplement*, August 25, 1932.
57. Beaumont groups Marino with those "luxurious Amoroso's," Theocritus and Ovid (*Psyche*, Canto IV, stanzas 110–11 [edition of 1702]):

> Whose consort to complete, aforehand came
> *Marino's Genius*, with a voice so high,
> That all the World rang with Adonis's Name.
> Unhappy *Man*, and *Choise!* O what would t.1y
> >   Brave Muse have done in such a *Theme as*
> >   *mine*,
> >   Which makes *Profaness* almost seem *Divine!*
> But . . . Thou stoutly scorn'dst to be in debt
> To any *Subject*, and would'st only ow
> Thy *Works* magnificence to thy vast Wit. . . .

58. Latin epigrams (Martin, 24, 37, 52); English epigrams (*ibid.*, 88, 95).
59. *Strage*, Bk. IV, stanzas 102–3.
60. A complete version, *The Slaughter of the Innocents*, was pub-

lished in 1675. The translator, an unidentified "T. R.," follows the text far more closely than does Crashaw.

61. Stanza 7 (Martin, 111).

62. Stanza 17 (*ibid.*, 113).

63. Book IV, stanzas 105, 83, and 107.

64. These metaphors come from a single poem, "La Canzone dei Baci" (Marino, *Poesie Varie*, ed. B. Croce [Bari, 1913], 21–24).

65. According to Sweetnam (*S. Mary Magdalens Pilgrimage to Paradise*, 107): "From flames of love, fountains of flowing teares sprang forth. . . ." The author of *Saint Mary Magdalen's Lamentations* (Lam. II) adds:

> My teares distilled from moisted eyes,
> Are rather oyle, than water to my flame. . . .

66. Martin, 307. Martin prints both texts of "The Weeper," that of 1646 (79–83) and that of 1648 (307–14).

67. On the other hand, another of the added stanzas strikes a note of deeper intensity than anything in the first version, and in its final and quietly piercing line, such a line as Vaughan might have written, arouses not applause but awe.

> Twas his well-pointed dart
> That digg'd these walls, and drest this Vine;
> And taught the wounded Heart
> The way into these weeping Eyn.
> Vain loves avant! bold hands forbear!
> The Lamb hath dipped his white foot here.

Indeed, this stanza, with its sense of profanation and of sanctity, comes nearer to moving the reader's emotions and to being religious poetry than anything else in this brilliant but somewhat chill performance.

68. Martin, 99.

69. *Ibid.*, 294.

70. Mâle, *L'Art Religieux après le Concile de Trent*, 65–72.

71. *The Golden Legend*, ed. F. S. Ellis (London, 1900), IV, 72–89; and Anna Jameson, *Sacred and Legendary Art*, I, 339–76.

72. Remond, *Epigrammata et Elegiae* (Antwerp, 1606), Bk. I, epigram xxix, 29. Cf. also references to the Magdalen madrigals of Marino (Martin, 433; and Wallerstein, 100).

73. On the Magdalen in French literature, cf. Brémond, *Devout Humanism* (*A Literary History of Religious Thought in France*, I, tr. Montgomery [New York, 1928]), 300–1 and note.

74. Representative Anglican poems on the Magdalen are those of Herbert and Vaughan. Joseph Beaumont's "S. Mary Magdalen's Ointment" (*Minor Poems*, 250–52) repeats the Catholic "conceit" of floods and flames. Isaak Walton, in an eloquent passage prefixed to his life of Herbert (*Lives*, ed. Bullen [1884], 259), calls St. Mary "that wonder of Women, and Sinners, and Mourners."

75. Remond, *op. cit.* Martin (*op. cit.*, 450–52) gives the relevant lines from the Latin elegies and indicates briefly their relation. For a more detailed study, cf. C. B. Mitchell, *The Translations . . . of Richard Crashaw*.

76. Of narrative poems and ballads inspired by Alexis, it is sufficient to cite the well-known eleventh-century version in Old French, the four Middle English versions of the fourteenth and fifteenth centuries, and the seventeenth-century Spanish *auto* of Balthasar Dios (cf. V. L. Dedeck-Héry, *The Life of St. Alexis*, [1931]). For the verses of Père Barry and the popularity of the devotion to St. Alexis, cf. Brémond, *op. cit.*, 167 and note.

77. Baring-Gould, *The Lives of the Saints* (1898), VIII, 413–20.

78. Martin, 337. The Alexias elegies first appeared in the 1648 edition, which, according to its title page, "added divers pieces not before extant."

79. Cf. the saint's autobiography, *Vida de la Sante Madre Teresa de Jesus*, 1562 (good translation by David Lewis); and Mrs. Cunningham Graham, *Santa Teresa* (new ed., London, 1907).

80. Mâle, 160–66.

81. *The Flaming Hart* (1642 ed.), 419.

82. Of course Crashaw must have known such Catholic litanies as that of Loreto.

83. Teresa, *Vida*, chap. I.

84. On the "wound of love," cf. Poulain, *Graces of Interior Prayer*, 144; on the stigmata of St. Teresa, Farges, *Mystical Phenomena*, 28.

85. The citations throughout this section have been drawn from the *loci classici* on the "wound of love": St. Teresa, *Way of Perfection*, chap. xix, and *Interior Castle*, Mansion VI, chap. 11; St. John of the Cross, *Spiritual Canticle*, exposition of stanza 9, and *Living Flame of Love*, exposition of stanza 2; St. Francis of Sales, *Treatise of the Love of God*, Bk. VI, chaps. xiii and xiv.

86. Cf. Warren, "Mysticism of Richard Crashaw," *Symposium*, IV, especially pp. 146–48.

87. The two phrases come from Herrick's epigram, "What God Is," and Vaughan's "The Night."

88. J. G. Frazer, *The Golden Bough* (one vol. ed., 1922), 356–59.

89. Matthew 27:45; Mark 15:33; Luke 23:44.

90. Selden, *Table Talk* (ed. W. S. Anson), 255 (under "Year").

91. Inge, *Christian Mysticism*, 104–22. Cf. also Joseph Stiglmayr, *Catholic Encyclopaedia*, V, 13–18.

   Though, in the sixteenth century, the authenticity of the Dionysian writings was suspect, Catholic scholars as trustworthy as Baronius and Bellarmine were their defenders.

92. Inge, *op. cit.*, 109, 106.

93. Other alterations in titles are significant: "Alexias" becomes "Sainte Alexias," and "In Memory of the Vertuous and Learned Lady *Madre de Teresa*" becomes "A Hymn to the Name and Honor of the admirable Sainte Teresa, Foundress of the Reformation of the Discalced Carmelites. . . ."

94. A stanza from Cosin's much abridged version runs:

> Christians are by Faith assured
> That by Faith Christ is received,
> Flesh and bloud most precious.

> What no duller sense conceiveth,
> Firm and grounded Faith believeth
> In strange effects not curious.

95. H. E. Wooldridge, *Oxford History of Music*, I (1929), 314–18.
96. "Adoro Te" and the other Latin hymns quoted are to be found in F. A. March, *Latin Hymns* . . . ("Christian Greek and Latin Writers," I), 1874. Cf. also R. C. Trench, *Sacred Latin Poetry* . . . , 3rd ed., 1874.
97. Martin, 292.
98. Wallerstein, "The Development of the Rhetoric and Metre of the Heroic Couplet . . . ," *Publications of the Modern Language Association*, L (1935), 166 ff.
99. Martin, 98.
100. Shafer, *The English Ode*, 128–57; Nethercot, *Abraham Cowley*, 136–38.
101. I am here indebted to Dr. Leicester Bradner of Brown University, who has allowed me to read his unpublished paper, "Irregular Latin Verse in the 16th and 17th Centuries."
102. Shafer, *op. cit.*, 146; Nethercot, *op. cit.*, 128–35.
103. Martin, 222–24 and 445 (note to p. 222).
104. The Latin quatrain (*ibid.*, 357); the English expansion (*ibid.*, 90).
105. *Ibid.*, 85.
106. Martin (126–30 and 328–31) gives both versions.
107. THE CHRONOLOGY OF CRASHAW'S POEMS. No part of Martin's work is more valuable than his methodical and painstaking investigation of the chronology (*The Poems of Crashaw*, lxxxvii–xcii), and most of his conclusions I accept as thoroughly sound. The "occasional" poems supply him with *terminus ad quem* dates; then the manuscripts are dated on the basis of the latest "occasional" poems contained within them.

The most useful manuscript, Add. MS 33219, an anthology, compiled for a lady, of Crashaw's best work in English up to 1634–35, includes all but one of the poems in the 1646 edition of *Delights of the Muses* (i.e., the secular poems). In 1635, he accepted a fellowship, which then implied celibacy; *circa* 1637, he became a priest. All circumstances converge to place the composition of all the secular poems, save some congratulatory addresses to the Queen, prior to 1635.

The Latin epigrams were written at Pembroke, 1631–34. Since Latin originals exist for all save three of the English epigrams, which are fewer in number and freer and more mature in style, it seems certain that the English epigrams are later productions; they may well have been written at Peterhouse. Crashaw's "Sospetto d'Herode" appears to have been written in 1637 (Martin, xci), and the Teresa poems between 1638 (cf. Warren, "Crashaw and St. Teresa") and 1647.

The second edition of *Steps to the Temple* (1648) professes, on its title page, to include "divers pieces not before extant." Some of the added poems, however, antedate 1646—e.g., "Ad Reginam," published in 1640 in *Voces Votivae;* the "Bulla," published in 1646 at the end of Heinsius' *Crepundia Siliana;* the poems on the decoration of the Peterhouse chapel; and, in general, the Latin poems, theological and secular, most of which appear in Tanner MS 465 and belong to Crashaw's years at Cambridge.

The new pieces, presumably written in Paris between 1645 and 1648, are all sacred poems in English and represent, obviously, Crashaw's style at its maturity: the odes ("O Gloriosa Domini," "In the Glorious Epiphany," "Charitas Nimia," "To the Name above Every Name," "To the Same Party: Councel concerning her Choice," and "The Flaming Heart"), the paraphrases of the Latin hymns, the Alexias elegies, and "Description of a Religious House." Apparently Crashaw's last poem, the ode to the Countess of Denbigh, "Against Resolution," was first published in 1652; a second, longer and otherwise different version, appeared, separately issued, in 1653 (cf. Martin, xlix and 348–50).

Since the dating of most poems cannot be more than

proximate, it is precarious (even though inviting) to conjecture the exact pattern of his stylistic development. If,
as there seems reason to think, the apostrophe added to
"The Flaming Heart," the ode on the Epiphany, and the
letter to the Countess of Denbigh represent Crashaw's
latest work, then he was moving away from Marinism.
Williamson (*The Donne Tradition*, 116–19) argues that,
through Cowley, the influence of Donne was reasserting
itself, but, curiously, omits mention of the "Epiphany,"
which, I agree with Miss Wallerstein, is Crashaw's most
"metaphysical" poem. The incipient change in poetic
style observable in the pieces cited may be due, I believe,
not to some "literary" influence but to an attempted change
in the character of the poet's religious life, a change represented by the turn from St. Teresa to Dionysius the
Areopagite.

A few general principles may be stated. As Lord
Chalmers first pointed out, Crashaw's line of development
was from Latin to English as a medium and toward an exclusive preoccupation with sacred themes. Stylistically, his
movement was toward looser forms, particularly the ode.
"The poems which were added to *Steps to the Temple* in
1648 show that . . . Crashaw's style was now developing
away from the clearly apprehended imagery and precise
metrical forms of his earliest poetry towards a freer verse
and a more complex metaphorical utterance, in which the
images, as in Shakespeare's later style, seem to follow each
other in quicker succession, without always being clearly
conceived or fully exploited . . ." (Martin, xci–xcii).

108. *Ibid.*, 244–45.
109. T. Campion, *Observations in the Art of English Poesy*
(1602), chap. II, "The Ineptness of Rhyme in Poesy";
Milton, prefatory note to *Paradise Lost*, on "The Verse."
110. *Biographia Literaria*, chap. XVIII. Coleridge's discussion of
the "origin and elements of metre" is germinal.
111. Yeats, *Essays* (1924), 195 ("The Symbolism of Poetry").
112. Cf., e.g., Sidney's "Apology for Poetry."
113. E. D. Snyder's *Hypnotic Poetry*, to which I am indebted,

treats a subject of much importance. Cf. also I. A. Richards, *Principles of Literary Criticism* (1924), 138, 143–44; and Max Eastman, *The Literary Mind* (1935), 177–82.

114. Martin, 327.

115. Cf. Richards, *op. cit.*, 199 ff. ("Badness in Poetry").

116. These terms come from H. W. Wells' admirable analysis of *Poetic Imagery*.

117. "I believe without any levity of conceipt, that hearts wrought into a tendernesse by the lighter flame of nature, are like mettals already running, easilier cast into Devotion then others of a hard and lesse impressive temper, for Saint *Austin* said, *The holy Magdalen changed her object only, not her passion* . . ." (Walter Montagu, *Miscellanea Spiritualia* . . . , 32).

118. Cf. intimations in Osmond, *Mystical Poets*, 118, and Watkin, *The English Way*, 287.

   Discussing "Conceits," Kathleen Lea wrote: "In his frequent use of the word 'nest' I do not believe that the image of a bird's nest presented itself to him. . . . For Crashaw we have an even longer list of words, such as 'womb,' 'tomb,' 'grave,' 'day,' 'death,' and 'fount,' which he used as it were ritualistically and in a colourless sense of his own. While it is proof of his greatness that he had this peculiar idiom of speech, it is also significant of his weakness that this idiom must be re-learned and explained." (*Modern Language Review*, XX [1925], 405.) This was a penetrating insight into the nature of Crashaw's poetic method; and it is the central merit of Miss Wallerstein's *Crashaw* that in some brilliant pages (especially 126–28) it develops and extends this thesis.

119. Cf. Warren, "George Herbert," *American Review*, VII, 258 ff.

120. "Fortunate man, you who may be said to be the father of your parent" (Martin, 222–23).

121. *Ibid.*, 286 (stanza 9); cf. "Charitas Nimia," *ibid.*, 280, and *ibid.*, 309 ("The Weeper," stanza 5).

122. *Ibid.*, 167; Herbert, "Employment."

123. *Ibid.*, 178.
124. *Ibid.*, 218.

> Flagrant sobria lilia.
> Vicinis adeo rosis
> Vicinae invigilant nives,
> Ut sint et nivae rosae
> Ut sint et rosae nives. . . .

125. On the lore of the eagle, cf. Phipson, *Animal-Lore*, 232–33.
126. Cf. "To the Queen's Majesty":

> Thou with the LAMB, thy Lord, shalt goe;
> And whereso'ere he setts his white
> Stepps, walk with HIM those wayes of light . . .

and the "Hymn to St. Teresa":

> A Golden harvest of crown'd heads, that meet
> And crowd for kisses from the LAMB'S white feet.

127. In my discussion of sensuous correspondences I am indebted to Miss M. A. Ewer's important *Survey of Mystical Symbolism*.
128. "Music's Duel."
129. "A Hymne of the Nativity" (Martin, 107):

> With many a rarely-temper'd kisse,
> That breathes at once both Maid and Mother,
> Warmes in the one, cooles in the other.

130. *Greek Anthology*, Bk. I, epigram 33. Cf. also epigram 34 (from Agathias Scholasticus): "Greatly daring was the wax that formed the image of the invisible Prince of the Angels, incorporeal in the essence of his form. But yet . . . a man looking at the image directs his mind to a higher contemplation. No longer has he a confused veneration, but imprinting the image in himself, he fears him as if he were present. The eyes stir up the depths of the spirit, and Art can convey by colours the prayers of the soul."
131. "On the Wounds of our Crucified Lord" (Martin, 99).
132. English epigram (Martin, 97).

CHAPTER FIVE

1. Here I am rephrasing a thesis from T. S. Eliot's already classic essay, "Tradition and the Individual Talent."

2. Warren, "The Reputation of Crashaw in the Seventeenth and Eighteenth Centuries," *Studies in Philology*, XXXI (1934), 385–409; and "Crashaw's Reputation in the Nineteenth Century," *PMLA*, LI (1936), 769–85.

3. T. S. Eliot, *For Lancelot Andrewes*, 125; Joan Bennett, *Four Metaphysical Poets*, 99 and 110.

4. The ablest discussion relating the noncontemporary author's meaning to the reader's is Louis Teeter's "Scholarship and the Art of Criticism," *ELH*, V (1938), 173–94.

5. Cf. the admirable essay on Crashaw (*The English Way*, 268–96) by E. I. Watkin, the Catholic philosopher.

BIBLIOGRAPHY

I. EDITIONS OF CRASHAW

Epigrammatum Sacrorum Liber. . . . Cambridge, 1634.

Steps to the Temple. Sacred Poems, with Other Delights of the Muses. . . . London, 1646.

Steps to the Temple . . . The second Edition, wherein are added divers pieces not before extant. . . . London, 1648.

Carmen Deo Nostro. . . . Paris, 1652.

A Letter from Mr. Crashaw to the Countess of Denbigh, Against Irresolution and Delay in Matters of Religion. . . . London, [1653].

Richard Crashaw's *Poemata et Epigrammata . . . Editio Secunda, Auctior et emendatior.* . . . Cambridge, 1670.

Steps to the Temple, The Delights of the Muses, and Carmen Deo Nostro. . . . London, 1670.

Poetry by Richard Crashaw. With Some Account of the Author; and an Introductory Address to the Reader, by Peregrine Phillips. London, 1785.

The Poetical Works of Richard Crashaw . . . with Memoirs and Critical Dissertations, by the Rev. George Gilfillan. . . . Edinburgh, 1857.

The Complete Works of Richard Crashaw, Canon of Loretto. Edited by William B. Turnbull. London, 1858.

The Complete Works of Richard Crashaw. For the first time collected and collated with the original and early editions, and much enlarged. . . . Edited by the Rev. Alexander B. Grosart. . . . 2 vols. [London], 1872.

English Poems by Richard Crashaw. Edited, with Introductions,

etc., by J. R. Tutin. Privately printed at Great Fencote, Yorks.,
1900.

Richard Crashaw. *Steps to the Temple, Delights of the Muses
and other Poems.* The text edited by A. R. Waller. . . .
Cambridge, 1904.

The [English] Poems of Richard Crashaw. Edited by J. R.
Tutin, with an Introduction by Canon Beeching. . . . London, [1905].

*The Religious Poems of Richard Crashaw. With an introductory
Study,* by R. A. Eric Shepherd. London, 1914.

The Poems English Latin and Greek of Richard Crashaw.
Edited by L. C. Martin. Oxford, 1927.

II. PRIMARY SOURCES

Andrewes, Lancelot. *Ninety-Six Sermons.* London, 1629.

Anon. *The Honour of Vertue. Or the Monument erected by the
sorowfull Husband, and the Epitaphes annexed by learned and
worthy men, to the immortall memory of that worthy Gentle-
woman Mrs. Elizabeth Crashawe. Who dyed in childbirth and
was buried in Whit-Chappell: Octob. 8. 1620. In the 24 year
of her age.* . . . London, n. d.

Anon. *Legenda Lignea: with . . . a Character of some hopefull
Saints Revolted to the Church of Rome.* . . . London, 1652.

Anon. *Parnassus Societatis Jesu.* . . . Frankfurt, 1654.

Anon. *Querela Cantabrigiensis: Or, A Remonstrance By Way of
Apologie, For the banished Members of the late Flourishing
University of Cambridge. By some of the said sufferers.* N. p.,
1647.

[Baillie, Robert]. *Laudensium AYTOKATAKPISIS, The Canter-
burians Self-Conviction.* . . . 3rd edition. London, 1641.

Baker, Augustine. *Holy Wisdom.* . . . London, 1876.

Bancroft, Thomas. *Two Bookes of Epigrammes and Epitaphs.*
London, 1639.

Bargrave, John. *Pope Alexander the Seventh and the College of
Cardinals.* Edited by J. C. Robertson. London, 1867.

Barksdale, John. *Epigrammata Sacra Selecta, cum Anglica
Versione.* . . . London, 1682.

Bauhusius, Bernardus, and Cabilliavus, Balduinus. *Epigrammata.* Antwerp, 1634, and Venice, 1711.

Beaumont, Joseph. *The Minor Poems of Joseph Beaumont, D. D., 1619–1699.* Edited . . . by Eloise Robinson. Boston, 1914.

————. *Original Poems.* . . . Cambridge, 1749.

————. *Psyche, or Love's Mystery, in XXIX cantos.* . . . 2nd edition. Cambridge, 1702.

Benlowes, Edward. *Sphinx Theologica* . . . (Sacred Epigrams). Cambridge, n. d.

————. *Theophila, Or Loves Sacrifice.* . . . London, 1652.

Bernard of Clairvaux. *St. Bernard's Sermons on the Canticle of Canticles.* Translated . . . by a priest of Mount Melleray. Dublin, 1920.

Bettinus, M. *Florilegium.* . . . 7th edition. Bonn, 1632.

Cabilliavus, B. *Magdalena.* Antwerp, 1625.

Carew, Thomas. *Poems.* . . . Edited . . . by W. C. Hazlitt. London, 1870.

Carre, Thomas. *Occasionall Discourses.* . . . Paris, 1646.

————. *Pietas Parisiensis, or a Short Description of the Pietie and Charitie commonly exercised in Paris, which represents in short the pious practises of the whole Catholike Church.* Paris, 1666.

Caussin, N. *Polyhistor Symbolicus.* Paris, 1631.

Chesneau, A. *Orpheus Eucharisticus.* Paris, 1657.

Cosin, John, editor. *A Collection of Private Devotions.* . . . London, 1627.

Cosin, John. *Correspondence.* Edited by Canon Ornsby. Durham, 1869–72.

————. *Works.* "Library of Anglo-Catholic Theology." Oxford, 1843–55.

Crashaw, William. *The Italian Convert . . . or the Life of Galeacius Caracciolus . . . Containing the story of his admirable conversion from Popery.* . . . London, 1639.

————. *The Jesuites Gospell.* . . . London, 1610.

————. *Manuale Catholicorum. A Manuall for True Catholickes.* London, 1611.

————. *Romish Forgeries and Falsifications: Together with Catholike Restitutions.* . . . London, 1606.

Crashaw, William. *The Sermon Preached at the Crosse.* . . . London, 1608.

Cressy, Hugh (Serenus). *Exomologesis.* Paris, 1647.

Donne, John. *The Poems* . . . *with Introduction and Commentary by* Herbert J. C. Grierson. Oxford, 1912.

Farr, Edward, editor. *Select Poetry, Chiefly Sacred, of the Reign of James the First.* Cambridge, 1847.

Fletcher, Giles. *Complete Poems.* . . . Edited . . . by A. B. Grosart. London, 1876.

Fletcher, Phineas. *Poems.* . . . Edited . . . by A. B. Grosart. Blackburn, 1869.

Floyd, John. *The Overthrow of the Protestants Pulpit-Babels* . . . *Particularly confuting W. Crashawes Sermon at the Crosse* . . . *Togeather with a discovery of M. Crashawes spirit: and an Answere to his Jesuites Ghospell.* . . . N. p., 1612.

Friedemann, F. T. *Bibliotheca Scriptorum ac Poetarum Latinorum Aetatis Recentioris Selecta.* Leipzig, 1840.

Gruter, Jan, editor. *Deliciae Poetarum Gallorum.* . . . [Frankfort], 1609.

———. *Deliciae Poetarum Italorum.* . . . [Frankfort], 1608.

Guiney, Louise Imogen, editor. *Recusant Poets. I. Saint Thomas More to Ben Jonson.* London, 1938.

Haeften, B. van. *Regia Via Crucis.* Antwerp, 1635.

———. *Schola Cordis.* Antwerp, 1635.

Harvey, Christopher. *Schola Cordis or the Heart of Selfe gone away from God; brought back againe to him and instructed by him in 47 Emblems.* London, 1647.

Hawkins, Henry, S. J. *Partheneia Sacra.* Paris, 1633.

Herbert, George. *The English Works.* Edited by George Herbert Palmer. Boston, 1905.

Hugo, Hermannus. *Pia Desideria.* . . . Antwerp, 1624.

Jonson, Ben. *Poems.* Edited by B. H. Newdigate. London, 1936.

Jonston, Arthur, editor. *Delitiae Poetarum Scotorum.* . . . Amsterdam, 1637.

Laney, Benjamin. *Five Sermons Preached before His Majesty at Whitehall.* . . . London, 1669.

Laud, William. *A Relation of the Conference between William*

Laud and Mr. Fisher the Jesuit. . . . Edited by C. H. Simpkinson. London, 1901.

Lloyd, David. *Memoires of the Lives, Actions, Sufferings and Deaths of those Noble, reverent, and excellent personages that suffered by Death, Sequestration, Decimation, or Otherwise, for the Protestant Religion, and the Great Principle Thereof, Allegiance to their Soveraigne, in our late Intestine Wars, From the Year 1637 to the Year 1660.* . . . London . . . , 1668.

Marino, Giambattista. *L'Adone.* Paris, 1623.

——. *La Strage Degli Innocenti.* Venice, 1633.

[Mayhew, Edward]. *A Treatise of the Grounds of the Old and Newe Religion.* . . . N. p., 1608.

Montagu, Richard. *Apello Caesarem.* . . . London, 1625.

Montagu, Walter. *Miscellanea Spiritualia.* . . . London, 1648.

Nostredame, César. "Les Perles, ou Les Larmes de la Saincte Magdeleine . . . ," *Pièces Héroïques.* Paris, 1606.

Owen, John. *Epigrammata.* London, 1624.

Panzani, G. *The Memoirs of Gregorio Panzani* (1634–36). . . . Edited by Joseph Berington. Birmingham, 1793.

Pona, Francesco. *Cardiomorphoseos.* . . . Verona, 1645.

Prynne, William. *A Briefe Survay and Censure of Mr. Cozen's his Couzening Devotions.* . . . London, 1628.

——. *Canterburies Doome.* . . . London, 1646.

——. *A Quench-Coale.* . . . Amsterdam, 1637.

Quarles, Francis. *Emblemes.* London, 1635.

——. *Hieroglyphicks of the Life of Man.* London, 1638.

Remond, F. *Epigrammata et Elegiae.* . . . Antwerp, 1606.

St. Ignatius of Loyola. *Exercitia Spiritualia.* . . . Edited by Roothaan. Augsburg, 1887.

St. John of the Cross. *Living Flame of Love.* . . . Translated by D. Lewis. London, 1912.

——. *A Spiritual Canticle of the Soul.* . . . Translated by D. Lewis. London, 1909.

Saintsbury, George, editor. *Minor Poets of the Caroline Period.* 3 vols. Oxford, 1905–21.

St. Teresa of Avila. *Interior Castle.* Translated by Benedictines of Stanbrook. 3rd edition. London, 1921.

St. Teresa of Avila. *Life.* Translated by D. Lewis. 4th edition. London, 1911.

————. *Way of Perfection.* London, 1911.

Sales, Francois de. *The Love of God.* Translated by Thomas Carre. Douai, 1630.

Sharland, E. C., editor. *The Story Books of Little Gidding.* London, 1899.

Shelford, Robert. *Five Pious and Learned Discourses.* . . . Cambridge, 1635.

Southwell, Robert. *Poetical Works.* . . . Edited by William B. Turnbull. . . . London, 1856.

[Sparrow, Anthony]. *Collection of Articles, Injunctions, Canons, Orders . . . of the Church of England in the times of Edward VI, Elizabeth, James and Charles I.* London, 1661.

Sparrow, Anthony. *A Sermon concerning Confession of Sinnes, and the Power of Absolution.* . . . London, 1637.

Stafford, Anthony. *The Femall Glory: or, the Life, and Death of our Blessed Lady, the Holy Virgin Mary, God's owne immaculate Mother.* . . . London, 1635.

Stradling, Sir John. *Divine Poems. In seven severall classes.* . . . London, 1625.

Suso, Henry. *Life of Blessed Henry Suso by Himself.* Translated by T. F. Knox. London, 1913.

Sweetnam, John, S. J. *The Paradise of Delights. Or the B. Virgins Garden of Loreto. With briefe Discourses upon her Divine Letanies.* . . . N. p., 1620.

————. *S. Mary Magdalens Pilgrimage to Paradise.* . . . N. p., 1617.

Sylvester, Joshua. *Du Bartas his Divine Weekes and Workes . . . translated and written by Joshua Sylvester.* London, 1621.

Torsellinus, Horatius, S. J. *The History of our B. Lady of Loreto. Translated out of Latyn, into English . . .* [by Thomas Price]. N. p., 1608.

Ussher, James. *Complete Works.* Edited by C. R. Elrington. 17 vols. Dublin, 1847–64.

Vane, Thomas. *A Lost Sheep Returned Home, or, the Motives of the Conversion to the Catholike Faith, of Thomas Vane.* . . . 2nd edition. Paris, 1648.

Vavasseur, Franciscus. *Theurgicon, sive de Miraculis.* . . . Paris, 1644.

Watson, Richard. *The Rt. Rev. Dr. John Cosin . . . His Opinion . . . for Communicating rather with Geneva than Rome.* . . . London, 1684.

White, John. *The First Century of Scandalous, Malignant Priests.* . . . London, 1643.

Wright, Abraham, editor. *Delitiae Delitiarum.* . . . London, 1656.

——. *Parnassus Biceps.* . . . London, 1656.

III. SECONDARY SOURCES

1. Studies of Crashaw

Barker, Francis E. "The Religious Poetry of Richard Crashaw," *Church Quarterly Review*, XCVI (1923), 39–65.

Beachcroft, T. O. "Crashaw and the Baroque Style," *Criterion*, XIII (1934), 407–25.

Bennett, Joan. "Richard Crashaw," *Four Metaphysical Poets.* Cambridge, 1934. Pp. 94–114.

Bliss, Geoffrey. "Francis Thompson and Richard Crashaw," *The Month*, CXII (1908), 1–12.

Chalmers, Lord. "Richard Crashaw: Poet and Saint," *In Memoriam Adolphus William Ward.* . . . Cambridge, 1924. Pp. 47–67.

Confrey, Burton. "A Note on Richard Crashaw," *Modern Language Notes*, XXXVII (1929), 250–51.

Eliot, T. S. "A Note on Richard Crashaw," *For Lancelot Andrewes.* . . . London, 1928. Pp. 117–125.

Falls, Cyril. "The Divine Poet" (Crashaw), *The Nineteenth Century*, XCIII (1923), 225–33.

Gosse, Edmund. "Richard Crashaw," *Seventeenth Century Studies.* London, 1883. Pp. 141–67.

Martin, L. C. "Crashaw's Brampston Epithalamium," *London Mercury*, VIII (1923), 159–66.

Mégroz, R. L. "Crashaw and Thompson," *Francis Thompson: The Poet of Earth in Heaven.* . . . London, 1927. Pp. 108–24.

Mitchell, Charles Bradford. *The Translations and Secular Lyrics of Richard Crashaw*. Wesleyan University thesis. In typescript. Pp. 175. Middletown, Conn., 1929.

Newdigate, B. H. "An Overlooked Poem by Richard Crashaw," *London Mercury*, XXXII (1935), 265.

Phare, Elsie E. "The Conversion of Crashaw's Countess of Denbigh," *The Cambridge Review*, December 2, 1932. Pp. 147–49.

Praz, Mario. *Secentismo e Marinismo in Inghilterra: John Donne. Richard Crashaw*. Florence, 1925.

Sharland, E. Cruwys. "Richard Crashaw and Mary Collet," *Church Quarterly Review*, LXXIII (1912), 358–63.

Tholen, Wilhelm. *Richard Crashaw: ein Englisher Dichter und Mystiker der Barockzeit. Das neue Ufer*, XLVIII (cf. *Year's Work in English Studies*, IX [1928], 206).

Wallerstein, Ruth. *Richard Crashaw: A Study in Style and Poetic Development*. Madison, Wis., 1935.

Warren, Austin. "Crashaw and St. Teresa," *T. L. S.*, 25 August, 1932.

———. "Crashaw, Catechist and Curate," *Modern Philology*, XXXII (1935), 261–69.

———. "Crashaw's 'Apologie,'" *T. L. S.*, 16 November, 1935.

———. "Crashaw's *Epigrammata Sacra*," *Journal of English and Germanic Philology*, XXXIII (1934), 233–39.

———. "Crashaw's Paintings at Cambridge," *Modern Language Notes*, XLVIII (1933), 365–66.

———. "Crashaw's Reputation in the Nineteenth Century," *PMLA*, LI (1936), 769–85.

———. "Crashaw's Residence at Peterhouse," *T. L. S.*, 3 November, 1932.

———. "The Mysticism of Richard Crashaw," *The Symposium*, IV (1933), 135–55.

———. "The Reputation of Crashaw in the Seventeenth and Eighteenth Centuries," *Studies in Philology*, XXXI (1934), 385–407.

Watkin, E. I. "Richard Crashaw," *The English Way: Studies in English Sanctity*. . . . London, 1933. Pp. 268–96.

White, Helen C. "Crashaw," *The Metaphysical Poets: A Study in Religious Experience*. New York, 1936. Pp. 202–58.

2. History, Academic and Ecclesiastical

Acland, J. E. *Little Gidding and Its Inmates*. London, 1903.

Albion, Gordon. *Charles I and the Court of Rome* (with a foreword by David Matthew). London, 1935.

Attwater, Aubrey. *Pembroke College*. . . . Cambridge, 1936.

Baring-Gould, S. *The Lives of the Saints*. 14 volumes. London, 1874.

Beaumont, Edward T. *The Beaumonts in History (850–1850)* (Joseph Beaumont, pp. 217–29). Typewritten copy in the library of Cambridge University.

Blackstone, B. *The Ferrar Papers*. . . . Cambridge, 1938.

Bodington, Charles. *Books of Devotion*. London, 1903.

Bowes, Robert. *A Catalogue of Books Printed at or Relating to the University Town and County of Cambridge from 1521 to 1893 with Bibliographical and Biographical Notes*. Cambridge, 1894.

Brémond, Henri. *Histoire littéraire du Sentiment Religieux au France*. . . . Vol. I, *L'Humanisme Dévot*. Paris, 1920.

Carr, J. A. *The Life and Times of James Ussher, Archbishop of Armagh*. London, 1895.

Carter, C. Sydney. *The English Church in the Seventeenth Century*. London, 1909.

Carter, T. T., editor. *Nicholas Ferrar, His Household and his Friends*. London, 1892.

Cédoz, Abbé F. M. *Un Couvent de Religieuses Anglaises à Paris*. Paris, 1891.

Collett, Henry. *Little Gidding and its Founder*. London, 1925.

Cooper, Charles Henry. *Annals of Cambridge*. 5 vols. Cambridge, 1842–52.

Davies, Gerald S. *Charterhouse in London*. . . . London, 1921.

Dedeck-Héry, V. L., editor. *The Life of St. Alexis*. . . . New York, 1931.

Dodd, Charles. *Church History of England, from the Year 1500 to the Year 1688. Chiefly with regard to Catholicks*. . . . 3 vols. Brussels, 1739–42.

Farges, Albert. *Mystical Phenomena. A Treatise on Mystical Theology in agreement with the Principles of S. Teresa.* English translation, London, 1926.

Feilding, Cecilia, Countess of Denbigh. *Royalist Father and Roundhead Son.* London, 1915.

Figgis, J. Neville. *The Theory of the Divine Right of Kings.* Cambridge, 1906.

Füllöp-Miller, René. *The Power and Secret of the Jesuits.* Translated by F. S. Flint and D. F. Tait. New York, 1930.

Gardiner, S. R. *The First Two Stuarts and the Puritan Revolution.* New York, 1886.

———. *History of England from the Accession of James I to the outbreak of the Civil War (1603–42).* New edition, London, 1894–98.

Gibbon, A. *Ely Episcopal Records.* London, 1891.

Gillow, Joseph. *A Literary and Biographical History . . . of the English Catholics. . . .* 5 vols. London, 1885–1908.

Guilday, Peter. *The English Catholic Refugees on the Continent, 1558–1795.* London, 1914.

Haynes, Henrietta. *Henrietta Maria.* London, 1912.

Herne, Samuel. *Domus Carthusiana: or an Account of the Most Noble Foundation of the Charter-House. . . .* London, 1677.

Hughes, Thomas. *Loyola and the Educational System of the Jesuits.* New York, 1892.

Hutton, William H. *A History of the English Church from the Accession of Charles I to the Death of Anne.* London, 1903.

———. *William Laud.* Boston, 1895.

Joly, Henri. *The Psychology of the Saints.* London, 1898.

Knowles, Dom David. *The English Mystics.* London, 1927.

Langdale, Abram Barnett. *Phineas Fletcher: Man of Letters, Science and Divinity.* New York, 1937.

Macleane, Douglas. *Lancelot Andrewes and the Reaction.* London, 1910.

Matthew, David. *Catholicism in England, 1535–1935. Portrait of a Minority: Its Culture and Tradition.* London, 1936.

Moeller, Wilhelm. *History of the Christian Church.* III. *Reformation and Counter-Reformation.* London, 1900.

Mullinger, James Bass. *Cambridge Characteristics in the Seventeenth Century.* . . . London, 1867.

——. *A History of the University of Cambridge.* London, 1888.

——. *The University of Cambridge.* . . . 3 vols. Cambridge, 1873–1911.

Nethercot, A. H. *Abraham Cowley: The Muse's Hannibal.* Oxford, 1931.

Osmond, P. H. *A Life of John Cosin.* . . . London, 1913.

Ottley, Robert L. *Lancelot Andrewes.* Boston, 1894.

Palmer, W. M. *Episcopal Visitation Returns for Cambridgeshire. Matthew Wren, Bishop of Ely, 1638–1665.* Cambridge, 1930.

Peers, E. Allison. *Spanish Mysticism: A Preliminary Survey.* London, 1924.

——. *Studies of the Spanish Mystics.* Vol. I. London, 1927.

Petre, Edward. *Notices of the English Colleges and Convents Established on the Continent after the Dissolution of Religious Houses in England.* Edited by F. C. Husenbeth. Norwich, 1849.

Phillips, G. E. *Loreto and the Holy House.* . . . New York, 1917.

Poulain, Auguste. *Graces of Interior Prayer.* London, 1910.

Richardson, Caroline F. *English Preachers and Preaching, 1640–1670.* New York, 1928.

Sharland, E. C., editor. *The Story Books of Little Gidding. Being the Religious Dialogues Recited in the Guest Room, 1631–32.* New York, 1899.

Skipton, H. P. K. *The Life and Times of Nicholas Ferrar.* London, 1907.

Teale, W. H. *Lives of the English Divines.* London, 1846.

Torry, A. F. *Founders and Benefactors of St. John's College.* . . . Cambridge, 1888.

Venn, John A. *Alumni Cantabrigienses.* . . . Cambridge, 1922–27.

Wakeman, Henry O. *The Church and the Puritans, 1570–1660.* London, 1887.

Walker, John. *Sufferings of the Clergy of the Church of England.* . . . London, 1714.

Walker, Thomas A. *Admissions to Peterhouse, 1615–1912.* Cambridge, 1912.

———. *Peterhouse.* London, 1906.

Watson, Foster. *The English Grammar Schools to 1660.* Cambridge, 1908.

White, Helen C. *English Devotional Literature: Prose, 1600–1640.* University of Wisconsin Studies in Language and Literature, No. 29. Madison, Wisconsin, 1931.

Willis, Robert and Clark, John Willis. *The Architectural History of the University of Cambridge.* . . . Cambridge, 1886.

3. Interpretations of Poetry and Other Arts

Alden, R. M. "The Lyrical Conceits of the 'Metaphysical Poets,' " *Studies in Philology,* XVII, 183–98.

Barroway, Israel. "The Imagery of Spenser and the Song of Songs," *Journal of English and Germanic Philology,* XXXIII (1934), 23–45.

Brooks, Cleanth. "A Note on Symbol and Conceit," *The American Review,* III (1934), 201–11.

Bush, Douglas. *Mythology and the Renaissance Tradition in English Poetry.* Minneapolis, 1932.

Cabeen, C. W. *L'Influence de G. Marino sur la Littérature Francaise dans la Première Moitié du XII*ᵉ *Siecle.* Paris, 1904.

Campbell, Lily B. "The Christian Muse [Urania]," *The Huntington Library Bulletin,* No. 8 (1935), 29–70.

Chasles, Philarète. "Le Marino: sa Vie et son Influence," *Études sur l'Espagne et sur les Influences de la Littérature Espagnole en France et en Italie.* Paris, 1847. Pp. 259–302.

Clark, Donald L. *Rhetoric and Poetry in the Renaissance.* New York, 1922.

Cory, Herbert E. *Spenser, the School of the Fletchers, and Milton.* Berkeley: University of California Press, 1912.

Craig, Hardin. *The Enchanted Glass: The Elizabethan Mind in Literature.* New York, 1936.

Croll, Morris W. "The Baroque Style in Prose," *Studies in English Philology.* Edited by K. Malone and M. B. Ruud. Minneapolis, 1929. Pp. 427–56.

Eliot, T. S. *Selected Essays, 1917–1932.* New York, 1932.

Ewer, Mary Anita. *A Survey of Mystical Symbolism.* . . . London, 1933.

Fry, Roger. "El Greco," *Vision and Design.* London, 1920.

Gosse, Edmund W. *Seventeenth Century Studies.* London, 1883.

Grierson, H. J. C. *Cross Currents in English Literature of the Seventeenth Century.* London, 1929.

————. *The First Half of the Seventeenth Century.* London, 1906.

Hirn, Y. *The Sacred Shrine: A Study of the Poetry and Art of the Catholic Church.* London, 1912.

Holmes, Elisabeth. *Aspects of Elizabethan Imagery.* Oxford, 1929.

Husenbeth, F. C. *Emblems of Saints: By which they are distinguished in Works of Art.* 2nd edition. London, 1860.

Jameson, Anna. *Sacred and Legendary Art.* Edited by E. Hurll. Boston, 1895.

Janelle, Pierre. *Robert Southwell the Writer: A Study in Religious Inspiration.* London, 1935.

Kane, Elisha K. *Gongorism and the Golden Age: A Study of Exuberance and Unrestraint in the Arts.* Chapel Hill, N. C., 1928.

Knight, G. Wilson. *The Christian Renaissance, with Interpretations of Dante, Shakespeare, and Goethe.* . . . Toronto, 1933.

Lathrop, H. B. *English Translations from the Classics.* University of Wisconsin Studies, No. 35 (1933).

Lea, Kathleen M. "Conceits," *Modern Language Review,* XX (1925), 389–406.

Leishman, J. B. *The Metaphysical Poets.* Oxford, 1934.

Levin, Harry. "John Cleveland and the Conceit," *The Criterion,* XIV (1934), 40–53.

Lewis, C. S. *The Allegory of Love: A Study in Mediaeval Tradition.* Oxford, 1936.

Mâle, Émile. *L'Art Religieux après le Concile de Trente.* Paris, 1932.

Mitchell, W. Fraser. *English Pulpit Oratory from Andrewes to Tillotson: A Study of its Literary Aspects.* London, 1932.

Myers, Weldon T. *The Relations of Latin and English during the Age of Milton.* Dayton, Va., 1913.

Osmond, P. H. *Mystical Poets of the English Church.* London, 1919.

Phipson, Emma. *The Animal-Lore of Shakespeare's Time including Quadrupedes, Birds, Reptiles, Fish and Insects.* London, 1883.

Praz, Mario. "The English Emblem Literature," *English Studies* (Amsterdam), XVI (1934).

———. "Romance Influences on Some Minor Caroline Poets," *Modern Language Review*, XX (1925), 280–94, 419–31.

———. *Studies in Seventeenth Century Imagery.* (Translation, with additions, of the *Studi.*) London, 1939.

———. *Studi sul Concettismo.* Milan, 1934.

Ransom, John Crowe. "Metaphysical Poetry," *The American Review*, III (1934), 187–200.

Ricci, Corrado. *Baroque Architecture and Sculpture in Italy.* London, 1912.

Saintsbury, George. *A History of English Prosody.* . . . 3 vols. Oxford, 1908.

Schirmer, W. F. *Antike, Renaissance, und Puritanismus.* Munich, 1924.

Scott, Geoffrey. *The Architecture of Humanism.* . . . Boston, 1914.

Shafer, Robert. *The English Ode to 1660.* Princeton, 1918.

Sharp, Robert L. "Observations on Metaphysical Imagery," *Sewanee Review*, XLIII (1935), 464–78.

Smith, James. "On Metaphysical Poetry," *Determinations.* Edited by F. R. Leavis. London, 1934.

Snyder, Edward D. *Hypnotic Poetry: A Study of Trance-Inducing Technique in Certain Poems and its Literary Significance.* Philadelphia, 1930.

Spencer, Theodore and Van Doren, Mark. *Studies in Metaphysical Poetry.* New York, 1939.

Spurgeon, Caroline. *Shakespeare's Imagery.* London, 1935.

Thompson, Elbert N. S. "Emblem Books," *Literary Bypaths of the Renaissance.* New Haven, 1924.

———. "Mysticism in Seventeenth Century English Literature," *Studies in Philology*, XVIII (1921), 170–231.

Underhill, Evelyn. *Jacopone da Todi.* . . . London, 1919.

Underhill, J. G. *Spanish Literature in the England of the Tudors.* New York, 1899.

Weibel, Walther. *Jesuitismus und Barockskulptur in Rom.* Strassburg, 1909.

Weisbach, Werner. *Der Barock als Kunst der Gegenreformation.* Berlin, 1921.

Wells, Henry W. *Poetic Imagery Illustrated from Elizabethan Literature.* New York, 1924.

Whipple, T. K. "Martial and the English Epigram . . . ," *University of California Publications in Modern Philology,* X (1925), 1–65.

Willey, Basil. *The Seventeenth Century Background: Studies in the Thought of the Age in Relation to Poetry and Religion.* London, 1934.

Williamson, George. *The Donne Tradition. . . .* Cambridge, Mass., 1930.

Wölfflin, Heinrich. *Principles of Art History.* Translated by M. D. Hottinger. New York, 1932.

——. *Renaissance und Barock.* Munich, 1888.

INDEX

ANN ARBOR BOOKS

reissues of works of enduring merit

The University of Michigan Press—Ann Arbor